0 = Never	
	1	

BRINGING HOME THE BACON

ALSO BY GINNY GRAVES

Pregnancy Fitness

As They Grow: Your Three- and Four-Year-Old

Harriet Pappenheim, L.C.S.W.,

and *Ginny Graves*

BRINGING HOME
the BACON

MAKING MARRIAGE WORK

WHEN SHE MAKES MORE MONEY

WILLIAM MORROW   *wm*   *An Imprint of* HarperCollins*Publishers*

The names and identifying characteristics of people featured throughout this book have been changed to protect their privacy. Any resemblance to actual persons, living or dead, is purely coincidental.

BRINGING HOME THE BACON. Copyright © 2005 by Harriet Pappenheim, Ginny Graves, and Roundtable Press, Inc. All rights reserved. Printed in the United States of America. No part of this book may be used or reproduced in any manner whatsoever without written permission except in the case of brief quotations embodied in critical articles and reviews. For information address HarperCollins Publishers Inc., 10 East 53rd Street, New York, NY 10022.

HarperCollins books may be purchased for educational, business, or sales promotional use. For information please write: Special Markets Department, HarperCollins Publishers Inc., 10 East 53rd Street, New York, NY 10022.

FIRST EDITION

Designed by Kate Nichols

Printed on acid-free paper

Library of Congress Cataloging-in-Publication Data

Pappenheim, Harriet.
    Bringing home the bacon : making marriage work when she makes more money /
Harriet Pappenheim and Ginny Graves.—1st ed.
        p. cm.
    ISBN 0-06-074754-4 (acid-free paper)
    1. Dual-career families—United States. 2. Married people—Employment—United States.
3. Marriage—United States. I. Graves, Ginny. II. Title.

HQ536.p364 2005
306.872—dc22   2005041494

05 06 07 08 09 RRD/JTC 10 9 8 7 6 5 4 3 2 1

For Wolf

—H.P.

For Marlene and Bill Graves, with love

—G.G.

Contents

BRINGING HOME THE BACON

A Quiet Revolution

A revolution is taking place in the lives of couples and families across the United States. It's a quiet one, but of cosmic proportions. Most women will talk about it only in whispers or when their husbands aren't around, and many men refuse to talk about it at all. But it's there all the same, silently transforming the American family, giving rise to new tensions, challenges, and opportunities within relationships, while, once and for all, laying to rest old gender stereotypes. Like most revolutions, this one is a product of its time and place, a complicated blend of evolving social mores and shifting economic realities, but it can be boiled down to a deceptively simple yet staggering statistic: Today, one in three married women outearns her husband.

Although the average woman's wage is still lower than a man's— she makes eighty cents for every dollar he earns—women are cutting wide swaths into traditional male careers such as business, law, finance, and medicine. In 1983 women held 34 percent of high-paying executive, administrative and managerial jobs. In 2001 women held nearly half of those senior positions. And it's a trend that shows no signs of slowing. Women are currently earning more college degrees and M.B.A.s than men, and they're entering medical school and law school in record numbers, clearly grooming themselves for plum, high-paying jobs, ones that very well may carry larger paychecks than their husbands'.

On its face, the fact that some women outearn their husbands doesn't sound like a combustible issue, especially in the year 2005. After all, women have been in the workforce for decades, and the fact that some of their salaries are starting to outstrip their spouses' shouldn't be particularly surprising, much less potentially explosive. But couples in the vanguard of this trend say the day-to-day reality of their paycheck gap raises complex and challenging issues.

This "modern" generation is caught in the thick of a paradigm shift, and our values and comfort level have yet to catch up with our new roles in the workplace and at home. When we first sought out couples in which the wife is the primary breadwinner, we wanted to get a sense of the issues at work in these new economic relationships. After only a dozen or so interviews, we realized that we were moving through a minefield. Even though this change in family life is widespread, it is so new that it evokes shame in otherwise strong and proud men and women. Most of the women would agree to talk only if their identities were cloaked. Moreover, many refused to even ask their husbands to participate, for fear it would be a blow to his ego. When women agreed to broach the subject with their husbands, oftentimes the men were not interested in talking to us. Those who were willing, however, shared their opinions freely, giving us an invaluable glimpse into the situation from the male perspective. It became clear after those conversations that even when the man is comfortable with his second-tier financial status—and there are men who have adjusted well—the role reversal has unexpected, sometimes unpleasant, ramifications in other areas of the couple's life, affecting everything from household chores and child rearing to spending habits and sex.

What's going on here? How could women and men who are open-minded enough to be living in such modern circumstances be hesitant or even downright unwilling to talk about it? What were they afraid of? Why does this issue create so much angst? And, more important, how could we help?

There may be a number of reasons for couples' reluctance to talk, but it seems the most basic one is this: When women eclipse men as the primary breadwinner, it can undermine both partners' fundamental sense of what it means to be male or female. Men who earn less than their wives often feel unmanned, and women who earn more worry that they'll be perceived as ballbusters, the quintessential emasculating female. Moreover, both partners' expectations of "women's work" and "men's work" are often turned on their heads, creating serious tension over other issues, like who does what at home.

From a biological perspective, some might argue that the issues run much deeper, all the way down into the very DNA on our chromosomes. Many anthropologists believe that since prehistoric times women have been programmed to find a mate who can provide for her children, whether it's by slaying a saber-toothed tiger or beating out a colleague for a big promotion. Although women without children may have participated in hunting, the theory goes that once she had a baby, a woman's role was to nurse and care for the child. In order to ensure their baby's survival, the primary goal of both father and mother, the man took over the role of sole protector and provider.

Modern men and women have made great strides in overcoming these ingrained attitudes and ideas, a tribute, anthropologists say, to our ability to adapt to new environments even if our genetic tendencies change more slowly. But society is changing at a lurching, one-step-forward, two-steps-back pace. In an ironic twist, the workplace—once thought to be hopelessly traditional and conservative—has been quicker to respond to the needs of women than the home front has, offering women opportunities that were unheard of even twenty years ago. While companies are becoming increasingly gender-blind, in the privacy of couples' homes, where women and men function together as partners, lovers, parents, and friends, roles and responsibilities are still often divvied up across strict gender lines. Despite the fact that women are out there taking on the same professional responsibilities as their male colleagues, they're still expected to be homemakers as well.

Researchers at the University of Michigan recently interviewed couples around the country to find out if the distribution of household chores had become more equitable. Happily, they found that men are doing more housework, five hours a week more, and women are doing fifteen hours a week less than they were thirty years ago. Impressive progress, to be sure. But the study's bottom line reveals a stubborn persistence within these gender stereotypes. The researchers found that women still carry significantly more of the household load, spending nearly thirteen hours a week more on things like laundry, dusting, and vacuuming, than their spouses, in addition to child care. And they're doing this on top of working outside of the home. A second recent study, by the Center for Research on Families at the University of Washington, painted a more disturbing picture: Those researchers found that the more money the wife makes, the more housework she does in proportion to her husband. Various explanations are possible. Maybe she feels the need to compensate for her success in the work world by being hyperfeminine at home, or perhaps her husband, whose masculinity has been rocked by his lower income, feels that pitching in around the house would be the ultimate blow to his manliness. Or maybe men have just become used to being mothered by women. What's clear from the findings: Even though the nature and rewards of women's work outside of the home have evolved with the times, "women's work" at home is still just that.

Housework and child care aren't the only areas of discord in these contemporary families. In talking to couples with "alpha earner" wives, as they've been dubbed in the media, we found that their financial situation often causes the entire family structure to undergo a tectonic shift. Suddenly everything from financial decisions to power and prestige is open to renegotiation and reinterpretation. Although some of these issues, particularly housework and child care, have long been hot buttons for dual-income couples (and have been well chronicled in everything from Arlie Russell Hochschild's groundbreaking *The Second Shift* to Allison Pearson's hilarious novel, *I Don't Know How She Does It*), they're clearly far from settled. And these touchy subjects take on a more urgent significance when the financial reins rest firmly in the wife's hands. Meanwhile, deeper issues, like power, prestige, pride, and shame, may rise to the surface for the first time when couples are challenged by their new financial roles.

Small wonder, then, that couples who find themselves in this new paradigm are struggling. With the basic titles of husband and wife unmoored from their traditional connotations, they're in limbo. Clearly the old identities—the homemaker wife, the breadwinner husband—no longer fit, but there is still no blueprint to follow to carve out new ones, and without a model, many men and women remain surprisingly resistant to change.

We interviewed more than one hundred people in this situation to get a comprehensive sense of the issues that arise when women make more money than their husbands. Because we wanted participants to be able to speak freely, without fear of being recognized by friends, neighbors, and colleagues, we have changed their names and identifying details. Most of our participants are college-educated and members of the middle or upper middle class—couples for whom the role reversal is new, not widely talked about, and often problematic. There are millions of couples in similar positions. (Many working-class women have been responsible for their family's finances for years, and the issues that arise, some of which are different from the ones we address here, have been thoughtfully analyzed in other places such as Jennifer Johnson's *Getting By on the Minimum: The Lives of Working-Class Women* and Barbara Ehrenreich's *Nickel and Dimed: On (Not) Getting By in America*.

Our sample is what is known in sociology circles as a "snowball sample," because we asked each person we interviewed to refer us to other people, and the group rapidly snowballed in size. As a result, it's not a scientific study but rather a slice of life, with representative stories from couples in their twenties to those in their sixties and from locations as far-flung as San Francisco, Salt Lake City, and Schenectady, New York.

Just when we thought we'd heard every permutation of the scenario, we'd talk to another couple who had a slightly different spin. The realization we came away with: No two couples' situations are identical, because each person brings a different perspective to the issue. Personality, upbringing, secret desires, and individual goals all play a role in how well men and women cope with their particular circumstances. But, perhaps more important, there are some striking similarities among these couples who are forging the new family frontier.

Many women who bring home bigger paychecks than their spouses enjoy what they do for a living and have always known they would be key contributors to their family's economic well-being. Indeed, some had their sights set on professional success from an early age, going to college, earning degrees, landing careers full of promise and opportunity, and proving through hard work and dedication that the glass ceiling is only so strong and can sometimes even be shattered with a well-aimed, deliberate blow.

When Caroline met David fourteen years ago, he was an executive earning five times what she made at her market-research job. But she loved to work, and although she took a year off after their son was born ten years ago, she couldn't wait to get back to the office. "By month eight I was restless, and by month twelve I was out of my mind," she recalls. She returned to work at about the same time her husband became a freelance consultant. While he has struggled to get his business up and running, her career has taken off. Now thirty-eight, she has an enormous amount of responsibility, with fifteen departments at her current company reporting to her—and the paycheck to prove it. "I wasn't built to be a stay-at-home mom," she says. "My temperament is much more suited to the work world. I love to get things done and to feel that sense of accomplishment."

Still, even some of the happiest wage-winners, including Caroline, are frustrated because their lower-earning spouses shirk their share of the housework, say, or spend money irresponsibly, another major issue for women who have newfound financial dominance. And when children enter the picture, even the most satisfied bread-winning wives may find themselves longing for shorter workdays, less stress, and more financial help from their partners.

When Katherine and Brian got married three years ago, Brian, now forty, was still a "big-income guy," working as a marketing director for a large firm, although he'd always aspired to be an artist, according to Katherine, thirty-seven. She had her own lucrative career as a creative director at an advertising agency, so although he earned more, they had a fairly equitable financial arrangement. Then, seven months after their wedding, he was laid off.

"We both figured, Oh, well, this will give him some time to do the painting he's always wanted to do," says Katherine. But as the months dragged into years and the couple had their first child, Katherine began to realize that, although she loves her job, being the sole family breadwinner isn't a role she enjoys or wants.

"Brian doesn't do much work around the house," says Katherine. "The way he makes a contribution to our family's welfare is by bringing home a paycheck. When he stopped earning a living, I began to feel like the family slave, the person who works all day, then comes home and does all the work around the house, and I'm tired of feeling resentful. I want to be able to spend more time with my son while he's young. I just want Brian to get a job."

Surprisingly, Brian, who is currently looking for work, is happy with unemployment, but that may have to do with the fact that leaving his time-consuming career freed him up to do the painting he loves. Men who have chosen low-paying professions they're passionate about—artists, writers, teachers—are less likely to feel paycheck envy than those who have lost jobs they strongly identified with or who are firm believers in traditional gender roles. And women who marry artistic types may be more willing to bear the brunt of the financial burden, especially if they knew from the beginning what they were getting into. Even so, some struggle with their partner's low-income status, especially if they secretly hoped that marriage would incite a "provider mentality" in their chosen mates.

Most women who inherit the mantle of breadwinner by default, who are forced to get a job because of a change in their husbands' breadwinning ability, are more conflicted about the role than those who chose the role of their own accord. Likewise, most men who are bumped from their financial throne, whether through bad breaks, cutbacks, layoffs, downsizing, or being outright fired, struggle with feelings of guilt, shame, inadequacy, hostility, and sometimes depression. After all, a man's identity, sense of power, and self-esteem have long been related to his work. Studies show that such dysphoric feelings may actually make men less likely to help out around the house with the traditional "women's work," a situation that can quickly push simmering tensions to a boil.

A March 2004 front-page story in the *New York Times* revealed that even retirement can be contentious if the husband chooses to opt out of the workforce before his wife, an issue that looms large in the coming years as baby boom men hit retirement age before many of their younger wives. In 2000, there were more than two million couples that included a man fifty-five or older who had not worked in the previous year but whose wife had, according to the article. Some older men who are trying to wind down become threatened by their wives' busy lives; others are eager to enjoy the benefits of retirement: the condo in Florida, leisurely days of golf, exotic travel—all plans that may assume the constant companionship of their spouse. Either way, when couples are out of sync, it causes problems, sometimes after years of marriage. In a study of older couples, researchers at Cornell University found that working women whose husbands were retired or disabled were the least happy in their marriages, while working men whose wives stayed home, the group that has always reaped the greatest benefits from marriage, were the happiest.

On the other hand, there is hopeful evidence of an attitude shift among the younger generation, couples in their twenties and thirties who grew up with the expectation that women would work, or at least could work, if they chose to. More younger men are choosing to step away from the family financial helm to be stay-at-home dads, and these men are sometimes much more sanguine about chores like housework and child care—indeed, many feel fortunate to have wives who can support them in their househusband roles. Randy feels that way. His wife, Abigail, is a copywriter, and although Randy has always made a little money tending bar, her income basically supports them. When they had their first child two years ago, Randy happily rearranged his schedule so he works only a few nights, allowing him to be a full-time dad during the day. "It's kind of unbelievable to me how much I like staying home," he says. "I love the fact that my children run to me when they get hurt, that I'm the one fixing them lunches and playing games with them. I'm constantly amazed at how natural it feels."

Promising as such stories are, men like Randy are still a minority. The Bureau of Labor Statistics says that in 5.6 percent of married couples the wife works and the husband doesn't. But that number includes men who are retired, disabled, or full-time students, so the actual percentage of men who are househusbands is still probably quite small.

Moreover, while Randy is perfectly content in the Mr. Mom role, many men in his position say they're finding some of the same frustrations—a lack of respect from the rest of society, for instance, and a sense of inequity over who does the household chores—that caused many homemakers-turned-feminists to rebel against the lifestyle in the 1970s.

Whether these husbands will stick it out for the long haul is tough to tell. But what is clear is that women will continue to bring home the bacon. And both partners will continue to feel ambivalent about their roles unless they find some guidance. The conflicts created by these new role reversals can lead to bottled-up resentment, tension, and anger that threatens to tear apart the relationship if it's unleashed, or slowly eat away at it from the inside if the feelings are pushed aside or ignored. It's a recipe for marital discord—discord that's become so loud, contentious, and common that it's spilled out from the confines of couples' homes and onto the covers of recent issues of *New York* and *Newsweek* magazines. While the media coverage has shown couples that they're not alone, it's provided only a fuzzy cultural sketch of what's happening. What couples really need is a road map to help guide them through this uncharted, often scary, territory.

We wrote this book to contribute to that guidance. We've uncovered the key issues that cause strife in these twenty-first-century households and come up with strategies to defuse the tension and address the problems. In the first two chapters we'll explain the underlying biological, emotional, psychological, and cultural reasons this financial transition is so difficult for most couples. In chapters 3 through 7 we offer targeted advice for helping men and women better cope with everything from housework and child-care battles to money, power struggles, and "sexless marriage" syndrome, a condition that plagues many dual-income couples but can be even more rife when women are the breadwinners.

This book is about money and how earning it (or not) can change the way you feel about yourself as well as your partner. But it's about much more than that. It's about relationships that are struggling for a variety of reasons, all of which are common, many of which are fixable. Most important, this book is about finding new ways to communicate and put aside outdated expectations so couples can learn to embrace their new financial roles.

The stakes are high, not just for those of you who are shaping this new approach to marriage but for your sons and daughters who will be looking to a whole new set of role models for guidance, and who will undoubtedly face similar issues and choices in their own adult lives.

ONE

The Man of the House

Paul was the kind of man Tom Wolfe would call a "master of the universe." He had a high-powered job in finance and worked long hours, sometimes seven days a week. He identified strongly with his role as provider, so although his wife, Ellen, had a low-paying job, he took care of most of their bills. While he made lots of money by most people's standards, he spent it lavishly, and he had dreams of living in real luxury, with a sprawling estate, lots of household help, and plenty of leisure time to enjoy it all. Then he lost his job.

That was two years ago, and Paul and Ellen have used up what little savings they had. Now they're trying to survive on Ellen's meager income. Paul's early attempts to find another job failed, and he has slipped into a depressive funk. He sleeps most of the day, and when he's not sleeping, he's often in a rage, his explosive anger the only thing that makes him feel powerful in what he sees as a hopeless, emasculating situation.

Then there's Steve. After scaling the corporate mountain for a number of years, he, too, had a high-powered finance job in his native Australia. Shortly after he married Kimberly, an American who also had a well-established career, they moved to the United States, and Steve left his hard-earned professional status behind. He started over in the States, though, and had begun building a thriving business in banking when Kimberly became pregnant. "We knew we didn't want our kids raised by nannies," Steve says now, several years later. They looked impartially at both their careers and agreed that hers probably had more upside potential. "Okay, I'll stay home," he said. "Kimberly didn't really want to give up her career," he recalls, "because it was really taking off, and I was willing to do it. I really love children, and although I felt a little anxious about leaving my job, this just seemed to make the most sense."

Why is one man incapacitated by the loss of a job and another, equally successful, man able to give it up willingly? Where does this male provider mentality come from, anyway? And how can twenty-first-century men who buy into the "Me Tarzan, you Jane" image ever reconcile themselves to playing a secondary role in the family financial hierarchy?

THE EVOLUTION OF MEN

Despite the fact that much of recorded history is an archive of men's thoughts and deeds (and far more of the latter), until recently not much attention was paid to masculinity itself, to how men define themselves as male or to what differentiates men from women. There are the shallow stereotypes—*men are macho and aggressive, they don't like to ask for directions*—but beyond the baritone voice, burly biceps, and five o'clock shadow, we know very little about who they are as a gender.

That seems to be changing. Thanks in part to the women's movement, which prompted deep and widespread analyses of the female condition, more experts of every stripe, from anthropologists to sociologists, are starting to look at the experience of being male, from prehistoric times to the present. With books as diverse as David Buss's *The Evolution of Desire: Strategies of Human Mating,* Michael Kimmel's *Manhood in America: A Cultural History,* and Susan Faludi's *Stiffed: The Betrayal of the American Man,* a portrait of men has begun to emerge that's far more complex and challenging than the stereotypes suggest.

During this tricky transition in modern marriages, when men are increasingly being unseated from their financial thrones, it's essential for women to try to understand who men are as human beings and why they react to things the way they do. Only with this understanding will it be possible for contemporary women to sustain a relationship with their male partners. With that in mind, we've taken a survey of the available literature to provide some partial glimpses into the male psyche—glimpses that can offer helpful insights to couples who are floundering in the swiftly moving cultural current of a gender-role shift.

Evolutionary psychologists, who study the prehistoric underpinnings of human behavior and emotions, believe that the most basic clues about what it means to be male lie in our evolutionary history. Men took on the role of provider for survival reasons. Those who were good hunters—who were muscular, strong, quick, and aggressive, who were good shots with a spear, and/or who had personal power within their social group and therefore were able to command a greater share of the communal food—were more likely to find mates. As a result, they also were more likely to pass along their genes than their less powerful, less dominant brethren, thereby begetting a whole new generation of virile offspring.

Generation after generation of natural selection eventually bred men who were not only physically larger and stronger than women but who were also eager to go on risky hunting expeditions, slay buffalo, and even compete against other men for limited resources (including women). Although humans are infinitely adaptable and able to change their lifestyle to adjust to their environment—scientists say we have our uniquely malleable and creative brains to thank for that—it seems to researchers more and more likely that the desire to support and protect a family is encoded in men's DNA. In the most primal sense, men may be programmed for hunting, or the modern version: providing financially.

As modern technology allows scientists to peer into humans' brains with greater accuracy, the results confirm what women (especially those women who have raised little boys and little girls) have suspected for a long time: that men and women are indeed wired differently. Like it or not, it's essential that women understand these differences and accept them. Many experts still tiptoe around the issue, however, because "different" has, in the past, been misconstrued to mean "superior" or "inferior." As Lisa Belkin writes in a 2003 *New York Times Magazine* cover story, "So much of recent history (the civil rights movement, the women's movement) is an attempt to prove that biology is not destiny. To suggest otherwise is to resurrect an argument that can be—and has been—dangerously misused." But men and women are different, and understanding and accepting our differences—as well as where each other's strengths and weaknesses lie—can help bridge the cultural and emotional chasm that separates the two genders.

Studies show that early in fetal development, the male Y chromosome triggers a cascade of changes that begins with the formation of testes, central headquarters for the production of testosterone, the hormone that sexualizes the male brain as well as the body. Under the influence of testosterone, babies' brains change in peculiarly "male" ways, affecting everything from the size of specific structures to the wiring of neurons, designed to enhance the flow of information. Studies show that the higher the level of prenatal testosterone, the smaller a toddler's vocabulary, a finding that could go a long way toward explaining women's greater verbal ability as well as the male reticence to "talk things out." There's also an evolutionary reason for women's enhanced verbal ability: Women didn't hunt, but they needed to communicate with other women in their family and/or social group. Women helped one another and one another's children to survive.

Another notable difference is that boys' brains develop more "white matter" (as opposed to gray matter), a substance that scientists believe may give men an advantage when it comes to certain spatial skills, like reading maps and navigating mazes. White matter may also make them more single-minded when it comes to solving problems. (We'll explain the advantages of female brains in chapter 2.) Numerous studies seem to corroborate this theory. By age ten, more boys than girls can rotate three-dimensional objects in their mind's eye, and at puberty, many boys begin to score better than girls on tests of algebra, geometry, and other subjects involving visual, spatial, and quantitative skills.

Although some experts argue that the testing discrepancies have more to do with the way boys and girls are socialized than with any true innate difference in ability, this is overly simplistic. Of course socialization has a huge effect on development, but we can never ignore biology. Evolutionary psychologists speculate that the capacity to think three-dimensionally may have come in handy during extended hunting expeditions, when the ability to scout and track animals as well as to find the way home after far-flung jaunts could have meant the difference between life and death.

Is it any wonder that men don't like to ask for directions? Why they think they can get someplace without a map? The fact that they seem to be spatially focused, thinking in larger frames of organization, may be one reason why men are not interested in "details"—a quality that can drive some women up the wall when, for example, they ask their husbands to make appointments for their children.

Why do men love using a metal stick to whack a little ball around a golf course? Are they using their spatial brainpower to chase modern-day prey? Why do they love hunting and fishing? Since experts believe that men went out in groups to capture and kill a mastodon or buffalo, why should we be surprised that men are enthralled and obsessed with team sports?

These biological clues to the origins of men's provider mentality are undoubtedly intriguing, but do they mean that men are hard-wired for work or more suited to today's workplace than women? Hardly, says Matt Ridley, an evolutionary psychologist. In his book *The Red Queen: Sex and the Evolution of Human Nature,* he points out that while our natural history may have primed men for hunting, neither gender is predisposed to be better at most of today's market work: holding meetings in a boardroom, putting together deals on a cell phone, examining patients in a medical office, or polishing widgets on an assembly line. Says Ridley, "The fact that 'work' became a male thing and 'home' became a female one is an accident of history."

The split between male functions and female functions on the homestead has been reinforced through the years, thanks to a number of economic and cultural realities. As Ridley observes, the domestication of cattle and the invention of the plow made gathering vegetables and grain—once the domain of women—a task that benefited from men's greater muscle power. And the industrial revolution of the nineteenth century accentuated the split even more, because for the first time "work" moved far away from the home. During this period there was a mass exodus of fathers from family farms, as men went to seek their fortunes in distant factories, while women stayed on the farm to nurse babies, care for young children, and tend the house.

Around this same time, attitudes toward "men's work" and "women's work" underwent a transformation as well. Some men began citing everything from religious doctrine to scientific and medical evidence that "proved" that women weren't tough enough, smart enough, or moral enough to enter the realm of paid work. According to sociologist Michael Kimmel, author of *Manhood in America,* this was an attempt for men, unaccustomed to punching a time clock and reporting to a hierarchy of bosses, to reestablish a sense of control, autonomy, and manliness.

Cultural ideas about fathering shifted around this time as well. In the eighteenth and early nineteenth centuries, the father was widely viewed as the moral overseer of the family and children. Fathers were responsible for children's religious training, for raising children to be moral adults. With industrialization and the relocation of paid work away from the home, this paternal role diminished. The father's contribution to the family came to be seen as primarily economic; the father once again became the hunter and provider.

HOW TO BE A MAN AND OTHER
LESSONS BOYS LEARN

Our interviews with dozens of men across the country reveal that the provider role is an identity many today still accept without question—and one that can be difficult for them to yield, even to a well-loved spouse. Although it's appropriate—even necessary—to expect men to change with the times, it's also reasonable to be sympathetic to their challenge. After all, it's really only in the last few decades—an evolutionary blink of the eye—that men have been asked to temper their aggressive tendencies and get in touch with their softer, more feminine side. It's only in the last decade that they've begun to lose economic supremacy within their own marriages. We're pioneers—something we need to bear in mind as we navigate this new terrain. It's also important to remember that our spouses are pioneering their roles as well.

As a man, you assume that you're going to be the breadwinner," says Duane, a fifty-six-year-old insurance adjuster in Atlanta. "When I met Ruth we were both in our twenties, and it never occurred to me that she would eventually earn more than I did. I would have been horrified by the idea, to tell the truth."

But Ruth, who had always been an independent thinker, went into mortgage banking, and she quickly rose through the ranks of her company. By the time they'd been married ten years, she was the dominant wage earner, and Duane was forced to rethink his ideas of personal success, marriage, and masculinity.

"It was tough," he admits. "For a while I was really jealous that her career was going so well, and I'd sort of take it out on her. I wasn't a very good husband, I'm afraid. Our marriage went through some rocky times."

Ruth is more blunt. "The issue nearly tore our marriage apart," she says. "My husband is the Marlboro Man—very macho. He's wonderful in many ways, but he really struggled with the idea that a woman, especially his wife, could make more money than he could. I tried to be respectful of his feelings, because I knew it was hard for him. But he'd pick fights and raise his voice at me. Finally, I said, 'Either we're going to counseling or I'm leaving.' "

Duane eventually agreed to see a marriage counselor, a move he says helped him realize that Ruth's income isn't an indictment of his masculinity. He now views their situation from a less personal per-spective. "We're in very different industries. No one in my business makes what she makes—not even the highest-paid people. I'm happy with my job and I'm good at it, and that's enough for me." But his grudging acceptance of their gender-role reversal goes only so far. "Around the house," he says, "she does the girl things—the cleaning, the laundry—and I do the guy things—the yard work and the handyman projects."

Even today, in an era several decades removed from the one in which Duane was raised, most boys are taught from an early age that they are what they do. The message comes from a number of differ-ent sources—the media, the examples of men in the community, their own fathers—making it all that much more difficult to ignore. Even the games many boys play as they're growing up—namely, competitive sports—teach them that the measure of a man is how well he can compete. "For many boys, making the team, from Lit-tle League to college, provides the ritual form of combat that is cen-tral to male identity," says Sam Keen, lecturer and author of *Fire in the Belly: On Being a Man*.

Dating back to the 1950s, TV-ready role models like the Lone

Ranger and his Madison Avenue–generated ilk (such as the Marlboro Man) created a one-dimensional image of masculinity—one in which the merest hint of femininity was suspect. Meanwhile, characters like Batman, Superman, and Spider-Man continue to shape boys' concepts of masculinity to this day. Young men, though often more flexible in their attitudes toward women's success in the workplace, still struggle to reconcile their own lives and significant relationships with those powerful, indelible early images.

"I spent half my childhood running around the house in a cape, pretending I was chasing down bad guys," says Colin, twenty-six, a graphic designer whose fiancée, a pediatrician, makes more money than he does, and almost certainly always will. "Even if you don't care about who makes more money, which I don't so much, you still have this idea that as a man you're supposed to be a superhero—strong, tough, invulnerable, almost. On the other hand, there's this new message from society, telling you you're supposed to have an equal relationship with a woman. Well, from a superhero's perspective, equal feels wimpy."

Boys' real-life role models, their own fathers, play another powerful role in shaping their gender identities. Indeed, a boy's father is like the übermale—the person he either models his own behavior on or reacts against, trying to become everything his parent was not.

Steve, the stay-at-home dad whose story we told in the beginning of the chapter, had a father whose work kept him largely absent from home, and Steve felt the void keenly. As he grew older, his attitude toward manhood was shaped by two conflicting views: that a man should work hard to provide for his family and that a man should be available to his family, playing catch with his kids and helping them with homework and the daily challenges of childhood. When crunch time came and Steve and his wife wanted to have a family of their own, he weighed the things that were important to him and realized that being a good parent—which to him meant an available parent (the thing his own father was not)—came out ahead of being a corporate power broker.

"I don't care if I have piles of money," he says. "At the end of the day, being a good parent and a good husband is so much more important." He adds a bit wistfully, "Was it difficult to give up the job? Yeah. I worked hard to get where I was, and I was damn good at it. But you have to make hard choices in life, and although it hasn't been easy in ways, I don't regret this one." Steve's idea that "good" parenting means "available" parenting sounds remarkably progressive coming from a man but actually has its roots in the 1950s. Fathers of the baby boom generation, alarmed by reports that the home had become too feminized and fearful that women were raising a generation of boys who would grow up to be sissies, were widely exhorted to reassert some masculine control around the house. The role models for the new participatory fathers were beamed into America's dens nightly on television shows like *Ozzie and Harriet, Leave It to Beaver,* and *Father Knows Best.* Even so, the central focus of manhood was still providing, as revealed in sociologist Talcott Parsons's 1959 comment: "Virtually the only way to be a real man in our society is to have an adequate job and earn a living."

People respond to their parents primarily in one of two ways: They repeat patterns—for instance, men feel they need to be providers like their own fathers—or they reject the role model, as Steve did in opting to be present for his kids, albeit unemployed. Obviously, a man's relationship to his own father and his experience in his family of origin will largely drive his comfort level with the nonbreadwinner role.

WHEN JOB LOSS EQUALS
IDENTITY LOSS

Job loss is a central theme in the stories of women who outearn their husbands; as the economic climate changes, more and more men are finding their careers cut short, their savings bled dry, and their long-term plans derailed. Reasons for the instability in the job market are myriad: The workplace is becoming increasingly technology-driven, pushing out many older workers who haven't been able to stay current, and making a number of jobs redundant; corporations are staggering under the dual blows of decreasing profits and increasing scandals; global competition is cutting into worldwide demand for American-made products; and the jobs that millions of men once counted on—the ones their fathers and grandfathers would have held for thirty or forty years—are increasingly being exported to cheaper labor markets overseas.

The net result is an increasingly hostile and uncertain work environment, one in which the term "job security" is becoming something of an oxymoron. The swaggering self-confidence of yesterday's providers, born in an era when a good job was virtually an American birthright (for white men, anyway), has been replaced by a subtle sense of insecurity, fed by the all-too-real fear of bringing home a pink slip instead of a paycheck. The impact of all of this economic uncertainty has hit men—who gravitate toward volatile fields such as finance and technology—much harder than it has hit women, who tend to work in steadier fields.

Timothy, fifty-two, a former trader on the stock exchange, was laid off twice within a few years, then decided to give up his fast-paced career to stay home with their two sons when his wife, Lisa, received a prime job offer in a new city. "Now I take care of the kids and do a little trading on my own, but it's not the same," he says. "I'd love to be able to roll back the clock to the nineties and be back on the floor, in the middle of the action. That was the life I loved, the one I always wanted."

Although Timothy usually tells people he's retired, the reality is, he couldn't get a job in his former industry today if he wanted to—and he knows it. "Guys like me are Luddites," he says. "Technology has altered the landscape so much that there's no longer a place for us. One of the great untold stories is that there are lots of men in my age group in the same boat. They say they're self-employed—the other popular euphemism—but what they mean is they're unemployable."

Although Timothy claims that he's never been "one of those guys who define themselves by their job," he admits he's never really hit his stride as a stay-at-home parent, either. "I enjoy being with the kids, but I'm not what you'd call a hands-on parent," he says. "I'm not Mr. Mom, anyway. I have good days and bad days. I'm taking a photography course right now and trying to keep busy. It's an unusual situation to find oneself in at this age, though."

It's hard to overestimate the impact of job loss. Married men who lose their jobs have a higher chance of getting divorced than their employed peers, according to a study by the National Bureau of Economic Research. Although the study didn't explore the reasons for the divorce rate, it's likely that it stems not so much from the loss of the paycheck itself but from the relay of consequences a job loss often triggers. When someone accustomed to feeling in control, powerful, and secure suddenly finds himself in a powerless position, it can wreak havoc with his self-esteem and his relationships with everyone around him. He can get depressed or angry or both.

Studies have shown that job loss for either a man or a woman is a powerful contributor to depression, social withdrawal, fury, relationship problems, and even deteriorating physical health. The loss of a job can mean not only the loss of financial stability but also a decrease in status and social support. It leads to self-blame and self-hatred, which is often turned against the partner in the form of nastiness, contempt, and even violence. A recent study conducted in California provides a dramatic illustration. The 2000 California Work and Health Survey, which showed that 20 percent of California workers had lost a job within the last three years and 10 percent had done so within the last year, found that people who were unemployed for an extended period were twice as likely to experience declining health and to become depressed as those who kept their jobs.

Financial strain is a key component of mental distress following job loss, but researchers at the University of Michigan identified another factor that plays a significant role in the downward mental and physical spiral: a declining sense of personal control. "Our results suggest that loss of personal control is a pathway through which economic adversity is transformed into chronic problems of poor health and impaired role and emotional functioning," the study's authors conclude.

Inga, thirty-three, who has a good job in marketing, has been grappling with the devastating results of job loss since her husband, Kurt, thirty-four, was laid off several years ago. When they met in 1997, he had a quarter-of-a-million-dollar salary in a high-tech field. "He was really good at his job and had been there for ten years or so," she says. The couple had a lavish wedding and bought an expensive apartment together in Manhattan. Then, shortly after they were married in 2000, Kurt received an even more lucrative job offer from a start-up company. "I urged him to take it," she says. "He'd always been one to play it really safe, and I thought it would be good for him to take a risk."

He decided to take the job, "against his better judgment" as he says now. Within a year the firm went bankrupt, and he's been out of work ever since. "He's become really down and depressed," she says. "He mopes around the house and does almost nothing. I can tell he's embarrassed and ashamed of his predicament, which I understand, but it makes it very difficult for him to talk about anything job-related. I think the male part of him is grieving what should be and he just can't make the flexible jump to what is. I keep pushing him to get any old job—even if it's selling DVD players at Radio Shack—but he has too much pride. He gets really angry when I even suggest something like that."

Although Inga's job is fairly lucrative, her salary isn't enough to pay their hefty mortgage and support their family forever, especially since they had a baby last year—"a big mistake," as Inga says. Since the baby was born, things have gotten so bad that Inga is worried her marriage may be heading toward divorce if Kurt doesn't find a job soon. "We have a big blowout fight at least once a week," she says, "and I don't want our son to be raised in that kind of household. If we're not happy, how can he be?" She adds, "I love Kurt, but I've lost a lot of respect for him, and I can't stand seeing him this way. I sometimes think it would be easier to be on my own, but the reality is, we can't break up, because what would he do? He doesn't have a dime to his name."

Without the "currency" of his income, Kurt needs to find other ways to contribute to the family and household—and Inga needs to be able to recognize and appreciate an alternative form of contribution, which is hard for her (and many women like her). Sometimes if unemployed men take over a good share of the child-care responsibilities, make dinner for their wives, and do the grocery shopping, their wives are grateful and, as a result, more patient as their husbands search for a job. Of course, all of this might be too emasculating for some men, who may just continue taking out their anger at themselves on their wives. Some couples may need the help of an objective third party, like a marriage counselor, to work through the hurt, frustration, disappointment, and resentment they feel, because often tensions are running so high that even starting a conversation without hands-on guidance is impossible. Even if Kurt does manage to find a job, he and Inga will have to work hard to heal the damage that's already been done to their relationship.

Given the overwhelming messages that boys have received through the years about the economic responsibility of real men, it's no wonder that losing a job—the starring role of a man's life as a man, and even more so as a husband and father—can deal a sometimes fatal blow to his sense of himself. But not all men sink into a depression when they're out of work. Perhaps their self-identities are more flexible or resilient, but some men are able to make good use of time away from work, even if work is where they'd rather be.

Mike, thirty-five, didn't actually lose his job, but he understands how frustrating it can be when you're trying to find work and not having any luck. When he quit his high-paying job in accounting in early 2001 to pursue a dream of competing in the Ironman triathlon, a grueling hours-long race that requires months of training, he had his finances well organized and his future planned out. "The plan was to take eight months off to train and do the race, then jump back into the job market," he says. "I'm not the type to make rash decisions. I had this all plotted out, and I decided it was a safe time to hit the pause button on my career."

During his time off, he met and fell in love with Stacy, who had a very high salary and a fast-paced career as an advertising executive.

Initially, he felt a little embarrassed admitting he wasn't working, but he made it clear he wasn't a slacker. "She knew my history," he says. "She knew I had a good degree from a prestigious university, and I think she realized I'd never do anything irresponsible."

He completed the race in early September, a personal achievement that was overshadowed several days later on 9/11. With the terrorist attacks, his plan of "jumping back into the job market" was thrown off course. "I began pursuing every job opportunity I could come up with and hoping that something would come through," he says, "but nothing was happening. It was very frustrating. I like feeling in charge of my destiny, and until that point, I always had. It was a very insecure, out-of-control feeling, but I just kept telling myself to hang in there, that things would eventually look up."

Although he wanted to ask Stacy to marry him, he was reluctant to do so until he had a job. "I didn't want to ask her to be my wife until I was able to show her that my life was on course," he says. "For a while there it felt like my whole life was on hold. It felt like I couldn't really move forward with anything until I got a job."

Through some diligent networking, Mike did eventually land a couple of consulting jobs, and while he was working on one, he proposed to Stacy. "I felt secure enough to do it at that point because I'd demonstrated that I had breadwinning ability with the consulting jobs," he says. "It was important to me to prove that not only to her but to her family. I didn't want my in-laws to think she was hitching her wagon to a bum."

Even so, when Mike and Stacy got married, he wasn't employed. "I was the houseboy," he says, only half jokingly. "I did the cooking, the cleaning, the grocery shopping, the bills—everything it takes to run a household, and Stacy brought home a paycheck. Some guys might not like that role, but I really enjoyed it. I'm a caretaker by nature, and I loved feeling like I was taking good care of Stacy in every way except financially. I derived a lot of personal value and self-esteem from that." For Mike, the currency that he brought to the relationship, though nontraditional, was satisfying to him, and to Stacy.

When Mike finally landed a job, nearly twenty months after the race, it was an adjustment for both of them. "We always joke that when I got a job she lost a wife," he says. Stacy still makes a good deal more money than he does, but he says it doesn't bother him. "Maybe it's because I wasn't employed when we first met or because of who we are as people, but we continue to see our marriage as a partnership."

What a contrast to Kurt and Inga. Mike and Stacy's relationship survived his layoff for a number of reasons, not the least of which is that they are two confident individuals who value each other and have remained friends as well as lovers. Because Stacy never had contempt for Mike's working status (and instead enjoyed having a "wife"/caretaker), and because Mike was willing to make other contributions while working to find a new job, these two were able to weather a prolonged bout of unemployment with very little strain.

MEN WHO CAN'T PLAY
SECOND FIDDLE

When Belinda, thirty-four, and Jeff, thirty-five, got married four years ago, he had steady work in construction and she had just opened her own small marketing firm. "He was the breadwinner at first, and he really liked that role," she says. Within six months, however, her business started growing—and her income grew right along with it. Now she has a staff of five and a thriving business. "We've won several awards, but Jeff doesn't even come to the ceremonies," she says. "He's tired of hearing about my success. The more I grow, both personally and professionally, the more he seems to be shrinking."

Jeff, for his part, has been "bugging" Belinda to start a family, but he feels they'll never be able to do that because her job is all-consuming. The tension between the two has become so unbearable that she asked him to move out several months ago. "Jeff was raised in a traditional family where his mom didn't work," she says. "Then his dad left and his mom really struggled. It's ironic, because one of the reasons Jeff always said he fell in love with me is because I'm ambitious and independent. He hated how screwed his mom got in her marriage." Recently, however, he's begun telling her, "The qualities I fell in love with are the things I hate the most now."

Jeff is studying to get his contractor's license, a move Belinda hopes will make him feel more self-confident and less threatened by her success. If it doesn't, she says, she's willing to let go of the marriage. "We've been together a total of twelve years, so it's a lot to walk away from," she says sadly. "But he needs to know that even if we have kids, I'm not going to stop working. I'm really proud of what I've built, and I'm not about to give it up—not for him, not for anyone."

Belinda's isn't the first marriage that's been torn apart over an income disparity. Paula, thirty-five, married James, sixteen years her senior, when she was just twenty-one. "He'd been to Vietnam, graduated magna cum laude from college, and was very charming, witty, and bright," she says. "He swept me off my feet." He also was the top salesman at a software company, where he earned an impressive salary, and she was a financially struggling journalist. By the time she was twenty-six, they had two children, and she left her job to do freelance public relations so she could spend more time with them. The move had an unexpected bonus. "I landed some lucrative clients, and within several years I was making well into the six figures," she says.

James's career, meanwhile, was faltering. "It was like he was intentionally tanking his career," she says. "He was being really irresponsible and losing clients right and left. Even though I was the one saving the family from financial ruin, suddenly everything I did was wrong in his eyes. He was very critical and could be really mean. He'd call me stupid, fat, ugly. I'm a lot of things, but those aren't among them."

They talked to a marriage counselor and came to the conclusion that the stress of his job was too much. So, in an attempt to save the marriage, they decided he should quit and, as she says, "try to get his act together." Instead of solving the problem, it exacerbated it, and their marriage quickly devolved into daily shouting matches followed by stilted silences. Two years ago she filed for divorce, a decision she doesn't regret, even though it's been hard on the children. "My income made him feel insecure and inadequate," she says. "He told me he thought I was mean and threw my success in his face, but I really don't think I did. I think the mere fact of my success was simply too much for him."

Unfortunately, James and Paula's therapist gave them the wrong advice, and now it is, sadly, too late to undo it. James's behavior was not the result of an external problem that could be fixed by quitting his job. Rather his problems—and those of other men like him, who feel threatened by their wives' financial dominance—require internal change. He needs to examine what's bothering him about himself and work to overcome those internal problems. The dynamic requires change on the woman's part, too, if she is in any way enabling his behavior. For whatever reason, men like James feel so helpless and unworthy that they regain a sense of power only by becoming furious, revengeful, and contemptuous. Paula shouldn't berate herself, because it's rare for any marriage to survive chronic contempt.

PIONEERS OF THE NEW MASCULINITY

With all the bad news about men and job loss, it may appear that patriarchy is in its death throes, but America remains a country predominantly run by males. Men still earn nearly 25 percent more than women for similar jobs, and they continue to dominate many traditionally high-paying fields, including finance, medicine, and law. Meanwhile, the power- and influence-wielders in our country—the media giants, the politicians—remain primarily male, primarily white.

Nevertheless, it's not, by any means, an easy time to be a man in America. While corporate America downsizes and goes economically global, so many typically male careers (manufacturing, banking, and technology, for example) have become less and less stable and men's old ideas about gender relations are being redefined in front of their noses. The notion of masculinity is up for grabs. Men have to find brand-new roles that suit how we live today.

For instance, Mike, the triathlete whose story we told in the last section, holds many old-fashioned ideals about manhood, and yet he is striving to create an egalitarian partnership with Stacy. In fact, in our interviews with men, the words *partnership* and *team*—male-sounding words with both corporate and athletic overtones—were used over and over by those who were the most satisfied with their marriages and most accepting of their wives' financial dominance. These partnerships don't need to be 50/50 divisions of labor and income. Rather, it's important that each partner contributes something valued by the other and that they are both working toward common goals.

Will, a social worker, and Tara have been married for ten years. From the beginning theirs was a fairly equitable partnership. Although they've known each other since they were children, they were reacquainted at their five-year high school reunion and were instantly attracted to each other. They started dating and it quickly became serious, but she was getting ready to move from their hometown in the Northeast to Atlanta for veterinary school. Certain that their relationship had long-term potential, Will "offered to accompany her and help support her through school," he recalls.

They got married, and once Tara graduated, they agreed it was Will's turn to choose where they would go. Before he had time to make a decision, however, Tara was offered a job in Pennsylvania. They both felt strongly that she should accept it. Within a year, Tara had decided to open her own office—a choice Will enthusiastically supported. Shortly thereafter she got pregnant, so although Will had started grad school himself, he quit so they could afford to get her practice up and running. "I didn't really mind quitting school," he says. "I'd already sort of figured out that what I was studying wasn't right for me anyway."

Now Tara's business is thriving, and Will is considering whether to quit his low-paying job to be a stay-at-home dad. "Financially it makes sense. I barely make enough to cover the cost of child care. But I don't know if I have the patience to stay home with a two-and-a-half-year-old. I'd really much rather be out in the work world doing something that earns a decent living. I'm very frustrated with my career, because there's just no potential to be compensated for the work. I don't mind that Tara makes more money—in fact, I'm delighted. I just wish I had more to show for the work I do. I look at Tara and me as a team with common goals. We both do whatever work has to be done—whether it's housework, child care, or making money—to see that we reach those goals. We have a very collaborative approach."

That doesn't mean their relationship is blissfully trouble-free. Will has felt very dispirited about his stagnant career prospects and the virtual impossibility of making more money unless he earns an advanced degree. But he's able to separate his personal disappointment from his feelings toward Tara's career. He realizes that the problem is his and not Tara's. He can't really explain where his egalitarian attitude came from, except that his mother always worked when he was a child. "My parents never really seemed to emphasize that traditional worldview very much," he says.

Will exemplifies another newly discovered trend in the wake of breadwinning wives. Although for decades wives have followed their husbands to jobs in new cities, studies show that women are now leading their spouses around the country. Data from the U.S. Census Bureau reveals that of the 13.8 million married female breadwinners in March 1998, 14 percent moved within a year. At the same time, among the 41 million male breadwinners who are married, just 10.5 percent moved.

A child of the generational shift that occurred when women began entering the workforce, Will is forward-thinking in his approach to gender roles. It's possible that, as more and more boys are raised by working moms, his attitude will become increasingly common. Of course, this depends on the quality of the relationship between the boy and his mother, and Will's seems to have been a positive one.

Our interviews seem to bear this out. Many of the men we spoke with who had less rigid views of gender roles had been raised by working mothers. Allen, thirty, a newspaper editor in a small town in the Midwest who earns about half what his wife, Alicia, a teacher, does, says, "I was raised by a very strong mother. She ruled the roost.

She was very strong-willed, and all her friends were as well. Men who were raised in more traditional households may feel differently when their wives make more money than they do, but my message to them is 'Get over it.' "

Several years ago, Allen was diagnosed with Crohn's disease, a potentially life-threatening illness. "That probably has something to do with my attitude as well. Life stopped being about money. I'm happy to be here and thankful for family and friends. I have career goals, but it's more important to me to enjoy the moment."

Through our interviews with men and women, we found some other common traits among men who value marital equity over male supremacy. While they often have jobs—sometimes ones that they care about deeply—their careers don't form the basis of their identities. This is a brand new phenomenon. It's hard to know all the reasons why this happening, but it's clear that a man's world is changing in significant and profound ways. With our volatile economy, men can expect to change jobs eleven times during their career, according to recent research. The old pattern of attaching yourself to a company for life and moving up as part of a team seems to be over for many men, making it harder for them to identify with the goals, leadership, and challenges of the companies they work for. Instead, they seem to be deriving a sense of fulfillment from a number of different sources, including being present, attentive fathers and helpful, respectful husbands. In addition, most are emotionally mature and able to look at their situation more objectively, and they have a strong sense of themselves as individuals, rather than solely as men. This is one of the most positive changes that we are witnessing. It's essential for the future viability of family life. What it means is that gender is not the issue. What is at issue is the kind of human being you are, the kind of character you have—and whether you have integrity, loyalty, and concern for your family and your fellow human beings.

In her groundbreaking book *Love Between Equals: How Peer Marriage Really Works,* professor of sociology Pepper Schwartz, Ph.D., found similar characteristics among her sample of husbands who were contented members of egalitarian marriages. She says that one common distinguishing factor among the men she interviewed was that "they liked children, looked forward to having their own, and wanted to be involved in the day-to-day upbringing of their family." But even more central to their identities was the fact that they valued the idea of having a deep, close friendship with their spouses, and they placed greater importance on that relationship than anything else, including the demands of work or kids.

Frank, forty-five, is one of these men. A former professional ice-skater, he met Leah, forty-eight, a litigator, when he was thirty-three and working in the communications department of a large firm. "It was the first time I'd ever dated someone who made more money than I did, but it didn't bother me," he says. "A lot of men wouldn't be comfortable with a woman like Leah because of her personal strength and professional profile. It would be easy to feel intimidated or emasculated by a woman who makes the kind of money my wife makes, but I don't compare our salaries. I've accomplished a lot in my area of expertise, and I'm proud of that." Here's a man with enough self-esteem not to be narcissistically injured by his wife's success. On the contrary, he is proud of her. Perhaps his self-esteem is even enhanced by the knowledge that he is married to a talented woman.

Interestingly, Frank was raised in a traditional father/provider, mother/homemaker household. "My role models were completely traditional, so it's hard to say where my attitude comes from," he says. "I think it was in me when I was born." Frank doesn't know why he feels the way he does, but he must have been raised to feel good about himself, enabling him to stand tall next to his wife without feeling overly competitive. This is probably in part the result of good and sensitive parenting, which he will likely pass on to his own children. Frank's attitude shows that it's not just role modeling that will facilitate this paradigm shift but raising kids with good self-esteem who are comfortable enough in their own skin to play numerous roles—even nontraditional ones.

Another sign of the changing attitudes of men is the increase (slight though it may be) in the number of stay-at-home dads or SAHDs, the new acronym. According to the U.S. Census Bureau's March 2002 Current Population Survey, among two-parent households there were 189,000 children with SAHDs. Though the figure is small compared with the 11 million children who are being raised by stay-at-home moms, the number of children living with SAHDs has risen 18 percent since 1994—a possible sign that attitudes toward male roles are changing.

Interestingly, some of the happiest SAHDs we spoke with combine their daddy day job with a macho side career or hobby. In a way, these guys may be saying to the world, "I may be a stay-at-home dad, but I'm still a guy." Randy, whose story we told in the introduction, is a bartender at night. Timothy, who used to be a trader, still gets up at the crack of dawn to play the markets. Then there's Clay. He happily left his job as a fact-checker at a magazine to take care of his two young children. "My wife, Sarah (a real estate broker), made four times what I made. We didn't have to do too much math to figure out who should stay home." But he's not sitting around the house watching television once the kids go to bed.

"I play poker several nights a week," he says. "I'm sort of like a semi-professional player now. I actually make a little money, and it's a nice balance to how I spend my days. I'm an avid reader, and I've really studied the game, so I guess you could say I'm into it in the same way some men are into their careers." The excitement for Clay comes from gambling, but his gambling appears to be under control. He and the other SAHDs profiled here have found healthy outlets for their needs for excitement, risk, competitiveness, winning, and control. Problems can arise if men who stay home with their children find outlets for these needs in areas that are destructive to family life.

Although many SAHDs have found a lot of satisfaction in their full-time parenting roles, they often still struggle with other people's attitudes toward them—proof that most of society hasn't yet caught up with the changing times. Steve, for instance, says that the mothers he comes in contact with often treat him as an anomaly, certainly not one of them, and many seem to view him as not quite competent, even though he keeps a spotless house, does all the gardening, cooks healthy, balanced meals, and is active in his children's school.

But he says his biggest problem is loneliness. "When I worked, other men always wanted to talk to me because they saw networking opportunities," he says. "Now I'm not an appealing contact." On the other hand, he's not accepted by the stay-at-home moms, or *muffia*, as Allison Pearson refers to them in *I Don't Know How She Does It*. "They don't know how to deal with me," he says. "I think some of them think I'm lazy and that I'm taking advantage of my wife, who's working hard day in and day out. I'm damned with the husbands, and I'm damned with the wives."

Says his wife, Kimberly: "It's a struggle, because he wants to be respected for who he is, not what he does. We're clearly not there yet as a society."

Even if men who've chosen to stay home with their children are accepted by their immediate friends and family—Randy the bartender says his guy friends come to his house once a week for lunch and they "get a kick out of" the fact that he stays home with his kids—they may get flak when they venture out into larger social circles. Call it the "cocktail party phenomenon." When a stay-at-home dad meets a new person, the inevitable first question ("What do you do?") can be a conversation killer.

Sharon, whose husband, Scott, has been a SAHD for seven years, since shortly before they had their first child, says, "That's the most difficult thing for a guy, because the whole issue of masculinity is called into question. When you don't have an easy business-card response to that question, it leaves both people feeling awkward. It's very hard for men to get over the sense that not having a job is something to be ashamed of. There has to be a way to admit to being a stay-at-home dad that honors the male ego." But we all know that child care was never an occupation valued by society—not for the women who did it traditionally, and not for men now. SAHDs have inherited a painful legacy.

Scott used to say he was retired, Sharon says, but that annoyed her, because he was only in his mid-forties so it sounded like they were independently wealthy. "He's finally gotten to a point where he can say, 'I take care of my children,' with his head held high. But it's taken a lot of emotional effort to get there."

Some men have managed to overcome even those entrenched stigmas. "I've never been invested in the idea of the macho man," says Johnny, thirty-seven, who has been a SAHD for the past four years. "I think of myself as very masculine. I'm a great baseball player and I love sports. But when I fill out a form that has a blank for occupation, I write 'homemaker' and I write it proudly. This is a hard job. If more men understood that, they wouldn't look down on those of us—male or female—who've chosen to do it full-time."

Men like Johnny may still be exceptions to the rule, but as their stories become more commonplace, attitudes in general will reach that mythical tipping point, and once that happens, all these ideas that now seem strange, unmanly, or threatening will, with luck, be accepted as simply a variation of normal. Until that day, our hats are off to men like Johnny, Steve, Randy, Clay, and Will, who've had the courage (a supremely "masculine" trait in itself) to create a new identity without the help of role models, like-minded peers, or widespread social acceptance.

TWO

Someone to Watch over Me

When Margaret and Richard first met nearly twenty years ago, they were both living in an artistic community in downtown New York. "We were part of the post-hippie generation—very into everything from art to equal rights," she says. "We didn't have much in the way of material things, but I didn't care. We had a very rich life of the mind."

On their first date, Richard, a musician, invited her over to his apartment and cooked her a delicious homemade meal. "I was very taken by the fact that he liked to cook," she says. "It felt so nurturing, like he was taking care of me."

Now in their late forties, they've been married fifteen years and have two children, both of whom are adolescents. Margaret, a personal life coach, supports the family while Richard makes a little money as a music instructor. He has spent the better part of their marriage, however, trying to make it in the music business—a career that has enriched him personally but has done little for the couple's bank account. Their economic arrangement, once a source of pride to Margaret, a staunch feminist, began to rankle her after they had their first child. "Before we had children, I didn't think about how much they would cost or how much I'd want to be able to spend more time with them," she says. "That came as quite a surprise."

What's been even more surprising to her is the fact that she feels Richard should take responsibility for providing the family's financial stability. "There's something about growing up with the fantasy of Prince Charming," she says wistfully. "I have this deep need to be taken care of—one that almost shocks me sometimes, it's so powerful. I have this irrational feeling that if Richard really loved me, he'd make more money and take better care of the children and me financially, so I wouldn't have to work so hard. He thinks my attitude is sexist, and I have to admit he's got a point."

But Margaret's attitude is not merely "sexist." It's biological, innately female, and instinctively maternal. Many working women (and nonworking women, of course) are shocked by the strength of their feelings when they give birth. It's impossible to anticipate the intense need to be with and care for children, or to imagine how guilty you might feel when you're at work instead of spending time with your kids. Although many women are content to work long hours when there are no kids in the picture, attitudes toward work change dramatically once there are other places these working moms would rather be. And if the subtext is "I wouldn't have to work so hard if he was making more money," then it's also natural to feel resentful of the person who is, however inadvertently, keeping you away from your children. These feelings are natural. But that doesn't make them healthy for a marriage.

Margaret and Richard are in no danger of going to the poorhouse, thanks to the fact that her career is so successful. "I only work twenty-five hours four days a week, and I make plenty of money to support us," she admits. "And I love my job. But it's very stressful and emotionally demanding, and there are many days that I'd like to be with the children but can't. I struggle with this feeling that I need to be in two places at once."

While she feels resentful of the fact that she is shouldering the responsibility for the family's financial well-being, Richard feels her resentment is misplaced—and unfair. "It's a strain, because Margaret would like me to be making a lot more money than I am," he says. "That's difficult for me to accept, because I'm an artist, and I have been one since she met me. She knew I was never going to be a captain of industry."

Both Margaret and Richard are right, and their feelings are natural and valid. The thing to remember is that marriage is a contract. It's important to be clear about the terms of that contract—especially in the beginning. And it's equally important to reevaluate and renegotiate the contract over time, as circumstances change. Margaret can't expect Richard to anticipate that her needs have changed since they had children. And Richard can't expect Margaret to accept that he's not going to earn much money because he never did in the past. They need to have an open dialogue about what each can contribute to the marriage—in terms of money, responsibility, and caretaking.

There are many ways that men can make their wives feel better taken care of that don't necessarily require a bigger paycheck. Some men take care of major projects around the house to reduce household expenses. Others take on the grocery shopping, cleaning, or administrative household duties so that their breadwinning wives can relax more during their nonworking hours. Margaret said that she felt nurtured when Richard cooked for her. The challenge is in coming up with an arrangement in which each partner can respect and appreciate the other's role.

Like the slain bison in prehistoric times, money is our modern-day form of security—security that we'll be able to put food on the table; meet the mortgage on the house in the nice, leafy suburb; pay for the kids' orthodontia; and provide opportunities for our own and our children's psychic, emotional, and intellectual development. On a deeper level, it's a buffer against one of our most primitive fears—of having no food or shelter, of starvation and exposure to the elements.

Just because women want to be taken care of doesn't mean that they want to withdraw from the world or regress into childhood. Most successful women couldn't imagine giving up their careers to be full-time moms and wouldn't want to rely on a man for total financial support. On the contrary, many women draw tremendous inner strength and self-esteem from their achievements at work and like the power of having their own money.

But after interviewing dozens of women who outearn their husbands, we've seen that the need to be taken care of may be more common (particularly once children enter the picture) than many women are willing to publicly let on. Fearful of looking like turncoats to the feminist cause or adding fuel to the conservative a-woman's-place-is-in-the-home fire, many women prefer to keep their dissatisfaction pent up, until they're like lionesses pacing a zoo cage. Or they'll air their frustrations privately with a few trusted friends. Whether it's articulated or not, it's very real—and needs to be addressed. Often men need to be reminded that their very independent, capable wives need tending to. It's up to you to kindly communicate your needs and suggest things that he can do (other than earning more money!) to make you feel taken care of.

PRINCE CHARMING: FANTASY OR FACT OF LIFE?

Just as women need to understand that men are unique creatures, so they need to understand themselves as well. A better grasp of the innate differences between the sexes will also help couples understand the magnitude of what they're up against (biology and hundreds of thousands of years of evolution) when the female partner brings in most or all of the money. Understanding the forces that drive men and women to think and feel the way they do will lead to greater tolerance, acceptance, and comfort with this "new order" of things.

Whether or not they realize or accept it, women do need to have someone watch over them because they are basically wired to watch over others—first and foremost, their own infants. This instinct to nurture is reinforced by their mothers, the rest of their female relatives, and society as a whole.

So if this need for "someone to watch over me" is all about maternal instincts, why do childless women have the same desire to be cared for? Probably because they, too, are consciously or unconsciously searching for the "hunter/provider." The difference is that breadwinning women who don't have children and don't plan to have children can usually handle an inequitable financial situation with some measure of comfort. (We'll talk more about the impact of children in these female-breadwinner marriages in chapter 4, Bringing Up Baby.)

Most women who have either chosen a mate who earns less or found themselves in the position of primary earner feel some ambivalence. Some mourn the lost chance to be taken care of. Some even feel that their breadwinner status makes them unfeminine. They may feel worthless and believe that their husbands don't really love them but are exploiting them or have married them for their money. It's important for women to work through any feelings of self-criticism and shame (ideally with counseling) for many reasons, including the fact that their marriages will suffer if they don't. The self-hatred can quickly morph into anger and resentment toward their husbands. As you'll see from the anecdotes throughout this chapter, these "pioneering" marriages are incredibly challenging, but what can we expect? We're in the process of changing an institution that has endured for thousands of years.

THE GHOSTS OF WOMEN PAST

Women today can be anything they want to be: bankers, lawyers, doctors, mechanics, to name a few. In the 1960s, Betty Friedan's *The Feminine Mystique* awakened a generation of housewives to the possibilities of life beyond casserole recipes and ironing, and they've responded by taking the work world by storm. While many women find deep satisfaction in their careers (indeed, for some, their jobs are as much a part of their identities as male careers have traditionally been for men), the mental shift from working woman to primary provider requires a quantum ideological leap that some have trouble making. It means giving up certain deeply held fantasies— of being cared for and protected *in a traditional way*. And it also means accepting the full weight of financial responsibility, with all its inherent pressures, time constraints, and emotional demands.

"I love my job, and I know I'll always work," says Terri, thirty-six, a medical-journal editor. "But when my husband was laid off last year and I was suddenly facing the possibility of being the only person making any money, I freaked out. Even though I feel very competent, I'm not ready to take on that much responsibility. And there's a part of me that really wants my husband to be out there along with me, working to pay our mortgage. Maybe I feel that's the manly thing to do. Fortunately, he found a job fairly quickly, so I didn't have to worry about it for too long."

But why on earth would Terri "freak out"? After all, most of the alpha earners we spoke with say they wouldn't want to quit their jobs and stay home full-time anyway. But they often wish their husbands' paychecks were more substantial so they could work less—or at least have the option to work less. Why do women experience this push-pull when it comes to paid work? And where does the unforeseen yearning for more support from their partners come from? As we mentioned earlier, some experts believe both phenomena may have their roots in the most remote recesses of women's brains, where the biological urge to nurture a child resides.

Anthropologists explain that, because pregnancy, birth, and child rearing require a large investment of time and energy, early women needed providers. As Helen Fisher, Ph.D., explains in *Anatomy of Love: A Natural History of Mating, Marriage, and Why We Stray:* "How could a female carry sticks and stones, jump to catch a hare, dart after a lizard, or hurl stones at lions to drive them from a kill—and carry an infant too? . . . Since the beginning of bipedalism, mothers needed protection and extra food, or they and their infants would not survive. The time was ripe for the evolution of the husband and the father."

Pairing up with men who were providers—who would put meat on the family table as well as offer protection from predators—meant that offspring had a much better chance of making it to adulthood, a goal that hasn't changed much through the thousands of intervening years.

Okay, you might be thinking, it makes sense that prehistoric women were naturally predisposed to find mates who would be steady, loyal providers. But the innate urge to find a male provider is one that has, in most ways, outlived its usefulness. After all, it's not like men are dragging home a freshly killed buffalo on the six o'clock commuter train. Why would that cavewoman mentality persist today, in a world where women are as capable as men of playing the provider role?

The attitude, anachronistic though it may be, has been reinforced through the ages by a number of factors, including economics. As we explained in the last chapter, the industrial revolution gave rise to an unprecedented division of labor—men worked in factories, women became housewives—that made money, and the power to earn it, a male prerogative. But even when women have worked outside the home, as they have off and on through the years, their financial contributions have almost always been deemed secondary to their husbands'. As a result, the unspoken quid pro quo of married women throughout history and across cultures and socioeconomic classes has been: I'll bear and care for our babies if you'll shelter, clothe, and feed our family.

Cultural messages have perpetuated the idea that a woman's place is in the home, even in our postfeminist world. From the time we're young girls, we are taught by our mothers how to be women and, more important, wives and mothers. The female-in-training lessons begin inadvertently with seemingly benign fairy tales and children's stories, in which women are often rescued from a life of drudgery (Cinderella) or eternal sleep (Snow White) by a prince, who is not only handsome and kind but also—and this, of course, is key—fabulously wealthy. Our heroine's future happiness and her financial security are assured—in fact, they're portrayed as one and the same.

As we grow older, the gender training continues in many forms, from how-to-please-your-man articles in women's magazines to romance novels and movies (remember *Pretty Woman*?). Meanwhile, the message that we need to rely on men for financial support was (and continues to be) subtly and not so subtly reinforced by our first and most important role models—our mothers. In the last generation, even if they worked, our mothers almost always played a beta role to the alpha provider, the father. And deep in the recesses of our mother's brains, no matter how alpha they themselves became, is the passionate commitment to the survival of their grown children and their grandchildren. How many women today secretly worry about the fact that their sons' wives are too busy working to take adequate care of their grandchildren?

"I'm the oldest child in my family and was raised to take care of myself," says Candace, thirty-four, an attorney with a prestigious, fast-paced urban law firm. Two years after graduating from college she took the LSAT, passed with high marks, and was wooed by some of the top-notch law schools in the country. She graduated with honors and landed a job at her current firm. Several years later she married Chip, her college sweetheart, who also is a lawyer. But he works for a small independent firm that doesn't pay nearly as well as Candace's. Now, after seven years of slogging her way up the firm hierarchy, she has fantasies of leaving her job so she can "be a wife," as she says. "I want to be able to cook and plan recipes and take care of the house. I don't mind working, but I'd like to have a career that allows me to be a homebody, too."

She and Chip have discussed their options if she were to quit her job. Since they don't have children, their choices are less fraught than for couples who are trying to save for college or pay for piano lessons. But they keep coming back to the same problem. "I make two thirds of the money," she says. "We wouldn't be able to meet our mortgage payment on his salary. It's frustrating and I feel resentful of Chip. I don't want to feel trapped in this career forever, but I don't see him ever making a lot more money. The only solution is to drastically change our lifestyle. I'm willing to do that, and he says he is, too. But I'm not sure he could. He's a real spender, and he's become pretty accustomed to my big salary."

The first thing Candace needs to do is to stop blaming Chip for trapping her. It's their lifestyle that is trapping her as well as her own conflict about depriving them of their spacious home, luxury vacations, et cetera. They have a big decision to make about how they want to live the rest of their lives together, particularly since they have no children. And when Candace makes that decision—whether she stops working altogether or takes a lower-paying, lower-pressure job—then she has to take responsibility for her choice.

In addition, it would be a good idea for them to sort out and formalize a financial arrangement so that Candace does not feel resentful of Chip's spending habits. If it's possible—as long as both partners are earning something—it's a good strategy to divvy up the household expenses (not necessarily evenly). This way both partners have discretionary income to spend as they please. (See chapter 6, "The Keeper of the Purse Strings," for specific suggestions for organizing your finances.)

WHAT DOES IT MEAN TO BE A WIFE?

While a number of writers, including Carol Gilligan, author of *In a Different Voice,* have lamented the loss of self-esteem that often strikes girls during adolescence, some research shows that our sense of ourselves as strong, independent, and capable is dealt a second blow at the marriage altar as we try to reconcile our personal aspirations with society's image of the ideal, Donna Reed wife. In *Mar-*

riage Shock: The Transformation of Women into Wives, writer Dalma Heyn cites the results of a revealing survey conducted in 1994 by *New Woman* magazine, which found that 83 percent of women believed that wives "submerge a vital part of themselves" when they marry. We can only speculate about why it happens, why we begin to deny our ability to take care of ourselves and stand on our own two feet once we're joined in holy matrimony with a man. But it happens to some of the best of us.

Candace's desire to "be a wife" sounds eerily reminiscent of the dilemma Colette Dowling portrayed more than twenty years ago in *The Cinderella Complex: Women's Hidden Fear of Independence.* In the following passage Dowling confesses to having let her writing career languish after she married her second husband: "In my mind he had become the provider. Me? I was resting up from those years of having struggled, half against my will, to be responsible for myself. What liberated woman would ever have imagined this? The moment the opportunity to lean on someone presented itself I stopped moving forward—came, in fact, to a dead halt."

This is a very complicated topic because many women are able to fulfill themselves intellectually and creatively within a marriage. It depends on the road they traveled before they got to the altar. Dowling was tired and needed a rest. Other women are tired of not being able to use work to express themselves individually.

Dowling was able to let her writing come to a "dead halt" because her husband had a lucrative career—he was, in the words of our mothers' generation, a "good catch." While the phrase sounds almost quaint today, the notion continues to permeate the culture of dating and mating, where a man's attractiveness is still very much tied to his earning potential.

Some of the most interesting evidence of this comes from a large-scale study spearheaded by David Buss, a professor of psychology at the University of Michigan and one of the foremost researchers in the field of evolutionary psychology. Over a period of five years, he and fifty collaborators around the globe looked at thirty-seven cultures to see how men and women choose partners, surveying more than ten thousand people in the process. His conclusion: Women the world over place a high premium on a potential spouse's financial resources. Men, by contrast, go for looks. In his book *The Evolution of Desire,* which explores the results of the studies, he writes, "Overall, women value financial resources about 100 percent more than men do, or roughly twice as much." Other studies show that American men who marry in a given year earn about one and a half times as much as men of the same age who remain single.

Buss's revelations dovetail with dozens of other studies, from the 1930s to the present. Researchers at the University of Washington in Seattle recently found that young women remain hesitant to marry men who are unemployed, even when the man is the father of her children.

It's easy to understand why middle-class and upper-middle-class women who live in traditional societies or who hold traditional values and expect to be homemakers rather than in the workforce would seek out men with fat wallets. But it's telling to note that the trend persists among today's high-earning women. Researchers at Bowling Green State University in Ohio found that college women who expect to earn the most money after graduation place *more* importance on the financial prospects of a potential husband than women who expect to earn less. Another study of female medical and law students, whose future incomes are likely to be substantial, found that they, too, rate a potential mate's earning capacity as one of the most important criteria for marriage.

Perhaps these women feel they'll be happier with men who, by virtue of their own earning power, aren't likely to be intimidated by their high salaries, or maybe they're simply acknowledging that they find ambition and hard work appealing, and those traits often go hand in hand with career success. But their attitudes could also reveal an underlying assumption that real men have big paychecks—an unspoken (and maybe even unrecognized) bias that could easily create tension and resentment in marriages where men earn less than their spouses. These are pretty powerful women we are talking about, and it's no surprise that they would favor powerful men. And in our culture, money means power.

"I liked being the boss's wife," admits Kara, forty-four, who had been a stay-at-home mom for ten years until her husband, Dan, a manager for a computer software company, was laid off in 2002. But when Dan lost his job, she quickly stepped up to the plate, landing a full-time position as a nurse, her former profession, with a local hospital just a week after he came home with the news. Although she says at first she "felt honored to be able to do something to support my family," the feeling wore off as the months of her husband's unemployment wore on. "I'm tired of people saying to me, 'Why doesn't he just get a job?' " she says. "A friend said to me recently, 'If that were my husband, he'd be out collecting grocery carts or working at 7-Eleven. There's no way he'd let me work while he sat at home.' Those kinds of comments really sting—especially because there's a part of me that agrees. I have to admit I've lost some respect for him since he's been out of work. I'm ready for it to be my turn to stay home again."

Inga, whom we introduced in chapter 1, wouldn't dream of staying home and giving up her career in marketing. "I have girlfriends who don't work, and they get very upset when the carpeting gets a stain or their new Corian counter is the wrong color," she says. "That attitude, to me, is a tragedy—that waste of brains and ambition. To me, a fulfilled life would be buying a new Corian counter and then writing an award-winning proposal on top of it."

Nonetheless, Inga is not really enjoying her stint as a breadwinner and is having a hard time concealing her frustration from her husband, Kurt, who has been out of work for three years. "He's so lackadaisical in his job search!" she explodes at one point. Although she appreciates the fact that he tries to pitch in around the house by grocery shopping and making dinner, she says, "I don't want my husband at home making scones. I want him out in the workforce, earning money so we can have the kind of life we both agreed we wanted."

In *The Bitch in the House*, a collection of women's essays, Sarah Miller addresses this sentiment with unapologetic candor: "There are few things that make a man less attractive to women than financial instability. We can deal with men in therapy, we can deal with men crying, but I don't think gender equality will ever reach a point where we can deal with men broke."

Both Kara and Inga are understandably angry—they feel helpless and frustrated. But pushing their men and getting angry at them is not going to be effective. First of all, men get terribly upset when women are angry at them, and they generally withdraw as a result. It's impossible to have a productive conversation with a withdrawn and silent man. And because job loss is such a devastating blow to a man's ego, all women in this position need to consider the fact that their husbands may be depressed—and that their depression may be prolonging their joblessness through a "lackadaisical" attitude and other nonproductive behaviors. Considering the volatility of the economy, and the fact that their husbands may need professional help, both Kara and Inga will need to be sympathetic. And coming from a place of sympathy rather than resentment, they will be better able to support their husbands' job searches, which will ultimately fulfill their own needs.

WOMEN'S MINDS, WOMEN'S EMOTIONS

The idea that women's desire to be protected and cared for may be partially a relic of evolutionary history, etched indelibly into our chromosomal code as a way of ensuring our safety, sustenance, and survival as well as that of our offspring, has received support from brain imaging studies. These recent studies reveal intriguing inborn differences between the genders—some of which may have evolved over the millennia to ensure that women would bond strongly with their mates as well as their youngsters.

Scientists say the female brain has 15 to 20 percent more gray matter and more densely packed nerve cells than the male version, anatomical differences that may help account for the fact that women seem to have a greater facility for language and are more adept at reading other people's emotions than men are. Both of those skills, in turn, may help explain why we're more likely than our partners to want to talk (and talk and talk) through issues. A story in the July/August 2003 issue of *Psychology Today* points out, "Females are gifted at detecting the feelings and thoughts of others, inferring intentions, absorbing contextual clues and responding in emotionally appropriate ways. They empathize. Tuned to others, they more readily see alternate sides of an argument. Such empathy fosters communication and attachment."

In fact, the latest psychological theories about women's development show that attachment is a key to our emotional health. For decades the prevailing wisdom in the field held that autonomy and self-reliance—essentially the male way of approaching the world—were the Holy Grail of mature adulthood. Over the last thirty years, however, a new theory of female psychology has developed—one that recognizes women's greater need for emotional connection within relationships.

Thanks to the work of Carol Gilligan as well as Jean Baker Miller, M.D., author of *Toward a New Psychology of Women,* we now know that the female tendency to develop close friendships, have deep, intimate conversations, and express feelings isn't a sign of neediness and insecurity but rather the hallmark of sound emotional growth, female-style. The problem is that women seem to think that they can have these intense, profound, emotionally laden conversations with their husbands, who, for the most part, aren't inclined toward that type of interaction.

In a 2002 study at the University of California, researchers found that women seek out other women, not men, in times of stress. The researchers speculate that in ancient times women needed to turn to other women in their social and family groups for protection and support on the home front while their men were away hunting. Women also needed other women to help care for offspring, which even today is a group endeavor, certainly in most cultures (although not so much in the West). An early woman had to bond with other females in the group so that there would be someone to ensure her child's survival in case she herself was disabled or killed. So the bonding of women to women is part of what women's propensity for intimate conversation is all about. Women are drawn to other women for support and nurturing.

It's not that men *can't* nurture. As a matter of fact, men today are much more attuned emotionally, more empathic and more interested in talking to women, than their fathers ever were. Yet men can never be expected to speak with a woman the way her girlfriends do. Women have to accept that reality and stop demanding daily heart-to-hearts with their men. It is really hard for guys, who in times of stress either fight or flee. And most men opt to flee or withdraw. Unfortunately, in Western cultures, working women with children who are part of nuclear (rather than extended) families have little time to schmooze with girlfriends, so their husbands are expected to pick up the emotional and conversational slack.

No matter how busy and overwhelmed you become, it's essential to make time to talk to female relatives or friends. Women need these interactions; it's crucial for them to be part of a community of women. To alleviate any guilt you may have about carving out time to be with friends, know that your mental and physical health actually depend on "girl talk" and therefore so does your ability to care for your husband and children. Whether you join a mothers' group, schedule lunches with girlfriends, or take a weekend away with another couple where the female is a good friend, female-to-female bonding in times of stress will go a long way toward preserving everyone's sanity.

CARETAKERS NEED CARETAKING

"I never believed for one second that someone was going to come riding into my life on a white horse and rescue me," says Leah, the high-powered litigator who is married to Frank, the SAHD we profiled in chapter 1. "My parents went through a very acrimonious divorce when I was twelve, and my mother told me I should never put myself in the position of being dependent on a man. I started working when I was fourteen to provide myself with new clothes and other basics, and I knew early on that if I wanted to go to college, I was going to have to pay for it myself. By the time I was an attorney in my mid-twenties, I was a little obsessed with paying my own way on dates. It was my own little litmus test. If it ruffled a guy's feathers, I knew he wasn't for me. That was one of the things I found so attractive in Frank. He wasn't intimidated by my career or my paycheck, even though he made much less."

Even so, after having two children, she now says, "My work is interesting, but Frank and I are starting to seriously consider our alternatives, because I feel so overwhelmed. I may try to make a career change, which would undoubtedly mean leaving New York City, the only place we've ever lived. My job is nonstop stress, and I work way too many hours. I get to work at 9 A.M. and race home at six-thirty so I can eat dinner with the family, give the kids a bath, and read them a bedtime story. Then I work in my home office for another five or six hours after they're asleep. The next day I wake up and do it all over again. I just want to work nine to five, but instead I have this little slavery thing happening. That's not what I had envisioned, even when I was younger and in my Virginia Woolf *A Room of One's Own* mode."

As Leah's story illustrates, there may be another, utterly contemporary, cause of women's desire for nurturing, for someone to sweep in and say, "Let me take over from here": exhaustion. Inveterate multitaskers that we are, many of us have simply added breadwinning to the long list of responsibilities we've always assumed around the house. We'll explore the division of household labor in greater detail in chapter 3, "The Home Front," but it's worth mentioning here that there is a limit to what we're humanly capable of accomplishing. The naïve and dangerous promise of the women's movement was that we could have (and do) it all. Most women who've tried know how futile that goal is. But the notion lingers, and it remains a central problem in relationships in which women outearn their husbands.

In support of this theory are studies of "his" and "hers" marriage, showing that the age-old institution continues to be more beneficial for men than for women, a finding that holds true today even though women are no longer restricted to the role of housewife. Although several studies have found that working mothers are happier and more satisfied with their lives than stay-at-home moms, other research has shown that working women are less satisfied in their marriages than their husbands. Working women also experience more stress from trying to juggle their myriad family and career roles and responsibilities. As Michael Kimmel points out in *The Gendered Society,* "The husband who works outside the home receives the emotional and social and sexual attention that he needs to feel comfortable in the world. His wife, who (probably) works as well, also works at home providing all those creature comforts—and receives precious few of them in return. Marriage may be good for the goose much of the time, but it is great for the gander all the time."

IT'S THE THOUGHT THAT COUNTS

Fortunately, there are hopeful signs of change on the horizon. In our conversations with couples in this situation, we discovered that some men who earn less money than their wives try to balance the marital scales by being caretakers in realms outside the financial one, and when they do, their wives tend to feel happier and less overwhelmed.

Karen, for instance, says that her husband, Al, is always looking for ways to lighten her daily load, from being emotionally supportive to doing chores around the house. "He tells me, 'I really appreciate how hard you're working for the family,'" she says. "He's genuinely blown away by how well I'm doing in my career. It may not sound like much, but at the end of a long, stressful day his appreciation and admiration really help. If I felt like he took me for granted, I don't think I could continue to work so hard."

Because he knows how tough it is on Karen when she has to travel, Al tries to do thoughtful things for her that will brighten her day when she's on the road. "I arrived at a crummy hotel in some no-name town recently and there was a big, beautiful bouquet of flowers in my room with a note that said, 'We love you.' Those kinds of gestures mean a lot to me. They tell me Al understands what I'm going through, and that in lieu of making more money he's trying to come up with creative ways to show his support."

Stacy, whose husband, Mike, was out of work for several years when they were dating and newly married (we told his story in the last chapter), says she always felt that Mike was protecting and providing for her, even though he wasn't putting a dime into their joint bank account. "When Mike was unemployed," she says, "he gave something more important than money to our marriage: tons of time. He cooked and cleaned and did the taxes and took care of the car and kept track of my frequent-flyer miles. It got to the point where I felt a little guilty, because I never did anything for him, except bring home a paycheck, which is something I did before I met him. He really went out of his way to take care of me."

Men like Al and Mike seem to have a natural nurturing instinct that helps them recognize the nonfinancial ways they can provide for their wives, and they're secure enough in their masculinity to be willing to take on those other responsibilities, some of which are traditionally female. But not every husband (or every wife) can readily discern how to meet his partner's needs. Human beings aren't clairvoyant, after all. We need guidance. That's where communication comes in. As Claire, a book editor, found, sometimes you need to tell your husband what you need in order to get what you want. "I don't mind making more money than Greg, but there are times that I'd love to have him treat me to things, just to make me feel cared for," she says. "I come from a very traditional family, where my father worked all the time and my mother stayed home with the kids. I remember him buying her jewelry when we'd go on family vacations or buying antiques for the house, because she really loved them. There was something deeply romantic about that to me, and I've always secretly missed that in my own marriage."

Claire was embarrassed to tell Greg, who makes a decent living as a newspaper reporter, that she'd like him to surprise her with gifts now and then. "It sounds so superficial and needy, in a way," she says—and she didn't want to "start a heavy discussion" in what was otherwise a happy marriage. So she kept her wishes to herself until the issue finally came to a head one day. "We'd gone to an auction and I saw this painting I really wanted. Greg knew I really loved it, but he didn't offer to help me pay for it—we keep our money totally separate—even though he knew I didn't have enough money to buy it myself. I was really hurt."

After giving him the "silent treatment" for a night, Claire realized she was acting childish, so she told him why she was upset. "I tried not to be accusatory," she says. "I just explained how I felt and told him that I would really love it if he'd surprise me with a little gift now and then. We can't afford anything extravagant, but it's not the price tag that matters. It's the thought."

To her delight and relief, Greg understood. "It was difficult to hear at first, because I like to think of myself as a thoughtful, considerate husband," he says. "But I know I'm not great about gifts. I think it might be because I didn't have a very good gift-giving role model growing up. I was raised by a father who bought my mom things like garbage cans and vacuum cleaners for Christmas."

Women who are bringing home the bacon are worn out, exhausted, and overworked. This is exacerbated for breadwinners who have children. Flowers, a kind word, or some other token of appreciation from the man they love can be incredibly important to them.

The problem is, many men don't know how important these "little" gestures are, so it's up to their wives to tell them. Although nobody likes to have to ask for gifts (and being put in a position where they have to do so can make women angry), language and tone are key here. If you ask for something in an accusatory way, it will put your husband on the defensive, alienate him, and create more trouble in the marriage than if you had never said anything. If he figures it out on his own, be sure to let him know how very much you appreciate his efforts.

In addition to the gift factor, which is tangible, Claire alludes to another significant issue for women: romance. When women are tired, stressed out, and angry, they don't feel very attractive—or attracted—to the men they love. As a result, often they are not behaving in a very lovable, attractive fashion. But women need to be validated as attractive and sexual beings anyway. When this happens, when a man tells his wife she looks pretty, kisses her unexpectedly, or even grabs her butt playfully—whatever romantic or sexual gesture he makes—it's likely to work like a magic wand, transforming the tightly wound "bitch in the house" into someone who's just happy to feel like a woman again. It's crucial that women understand that they have this need. And again, know that you may need to communicate your needs to your partner. (We'll discuss this in greater detail in chapter 5, "Couple Time.")

REDEFINING THE MEANING OF SUCCESS

Science has proven what both men and women have known all along: that women think differently, behave differently, and have different emotional needs than men. Now further research seems to indicate that women's interpretations of success may be much more broad, meandering, and diverse than the traditional unwavering ascent up the corporate ladder offered by the work world, a factor that can compound the turmoil in marriages where women make the bulk of the money.

"I expect I'll probably be made partner by the end of the year," says Candace, the attorney we mentioned earlier. Instead of sounding delighted, however, her voice has a note of dejection. "It's true," she admits. "I'm not excited about it. I really don't like my job. I like that I'm good at it, but I feel sort of trapped by my success. You grow up believing that if you're good at something that's what you should do, but my career is so time-consuming it doesn't really allow me to have a life outside work. I never wanted that kind of total commitment."

As Candace sees it, if she's made partner, her future is sealed and she'll never be able to break free from the demands of her career. "I know myself," she says. "I've always been very determined. If I become a partner, I'll expect myself to be the best partner I can be."

It seems astounding that after years of striving to reach the upper echelons of the corporate hierarchy, any woman would become disillusioned when she's on the cusp of reaching that goal. But studies show that Candace isn't an anomaly. A recent survey by Catalyst, a nonprofit research company focusing on women and work, found that 26 percent of women on the verge of being promoted to the top tiers of their companies don't want the job. The corporate door is open, the welcome mat is neatly laid out. So why are these go-getters turning away at the threshold? There's some evidence they're heading for home, or at least back down the ladder a few rungs, where home isn't so many worlds away.

A *Time* magazine cover story in March 2004, which ran under the inflammatory title "The Case for Staying Home," documents the trend. According to the article, the proportion of working married mothers with children under age three dropped from 61 percent in 1997 to 58 percent in 2002—the first decline of its kind since women began storming the workplace thirty years ago. The dip was mostly among women who were white, over thirty, and well educated—those who are economically secure enough to have a choice in the matter. If putting food on the table weren't a consideration for millions of other, less privileged, women, it's possible that the numbers would be much higher. The brass ring these successful career women are aiming for clearly isn't a prestigious promotion, more zeroes on their paycheck, or greater clout in the boardroom. It's a more subtle, elusive, and—dare we say it?—feminine goal: balance.

When Karen and Al met sixteen years ago, they were both working in real estate investment. Several years later, shortly after they were married, Karen took a job in a high-tech field and Al went out on his own, starting a real estate development company. He made money sporadically, but the business never really took off. Her career, meanwhile, was on a meteoric trajectory. "I now manage a two-hundred-million-dollar business and three hundred employees," she says, sounding somewhat awestruck by this reality. "My career is a big part of my personality. Even if Al struck it rich, it's hard to imagine I'd quit."

What Karen can imagine, however—in fact what she fantasizes about almost daily—is cutting back. With their two children now seven and nine, she feels the invisible cord drawing her home more strongly than ever. "When they were little there was a lot of physical juggling—breast feeding, getting them to day care—but I found it pretty manageable," she says. "Now they have these intense emotional needs. My nine-year-old son said to me this morning, 'You're not going on a business trip again today, are you?' I feel how much he needs me right now, and that makes it very difficult to walk out the door."

In an ideal world, Karen says, she and Al would have a more equitable financial arrangement—he'd earn more, she'd earn less—so she would feel less pressured and more able to cut back on her hours. "I'd like to work fewer hours and travel less," she says. "My career feels so relentless right now, like I'm on a treadmill with no end in sight. I just wish it felt more optional."

In truth, Karen is probably rich enough to have options, but she is deeply divided within herself. The pleasure, the self-esteem, and the sense of empowerment she feels with her professional successes are very hard to give up. She will need to acknowledge this so that she doesn't grow resentful of Al. She can choose to keep working—even at the same hectic pace—if she wants, but she needs to know that the guilt goes with the job. It's the price that women (though not men) often have to pay for professional success. So if she does continue working this same way, she'll also need to find ways to cope with her guilt.

Women's hunger for options, for leeway, for relief from the relentless grind, were recurrent themes in our interviews. Perhaps when women pine for a male provider, what they're really craving is greater latitude in a life that's come to feel too restrictive. What's clear is that when a career becomes just another kind of trap, limiting our options, dictating the course of our lives, many of us become disenchanted and start trying to find a way out. If there's one trait that characterizes the new postfeminist movement, it's the desire for choice—in everything from whether to keep a pregnancy to whether to be a career woman, a full-time mother, or some combination of the two.

It's possible (maybe even probable) that male breadwinners feel the same way about being trapped in the daily grind, but unless they are very wealthy, it never occurs to the majority of them that they have an option to stop working. Men might start looking for a new job, but if they can't get one and they have a family to support, they usually stay where they are, like it or not. They certainly don't seriously feel that they are entitled to be taken care of by their wives. But many women, consciously or unconsciously, feel entitled to be taken care of by their men. The sooner women realize that this is what's going on inside them, the sooner they can come to terms with their resentment and acknowledge that times have changed, and that they have made a different bargain in a brand-new world.

DIFFERENT SITUATIONS CALL FOR DIFFERENT SOLUTIONS

For some women, the need for change in their marriage goes deeper than caring gestures or thoughtful gifts. Women who feel deeply dissatisfied with the status quo may want to consider more serious measures to restore some balance to their overburdened lives.

For Jill, thirty-eight, a partner in a law firm, that meant going to her partners and telling them she no longer wanted to work on Fridays, so she could spend more time with her family. Her husband, Johnny, whom we mentioned in the last chapter, is a stay-at-home dad. "I'm a type-A person," she says. "I definitely belong in the work world, so it was a difficult choice to make. Saying you want to work eighty percent of the time for eighty percent of the pay is often career suicide in this field, but it was really for my peace of mind. I think it's different for women who are breadwinners than for the men who played that role for years. I have second thoughts about being away from home, because I know what I'm missing. I'm not willing to do a total role reversal and never see my family. That's too much of a sacrifice." Jill's desire to see her children is perfectly normal—and it's great that she could see that, orchestrate it, and not beat herself up over whatever repercussions may befall her in the workplace.

Jane, forty-one, a corporate image consultant and born-and-bred New Yorker, and her husband, Kevin, a graphic designer, took what was for them an even more drastic step: they moved to the suburbs. "My identity was very linked to being a New Yorker," she says, "so it was hard for me to leave, and almost as hard for me to think about raising my two children in suburbia. But in the city we felt like we had to send the kids to private school, because the public ones aren't very good, and it was costing us twenty thousand dollars a year for each child." Their combined incomes are high, but even so, with the cost of their mortgage and day-to-day expenses, the urban lifestyle was bleeding their bank accounts dry.

"We moved largely so we could bring our expenses down," Jane says. "I don't know that I want to stay at this job forever, so this gives me a little more freedom to consider my options." The move was effective—to a point. "Financially, I feel less burdened," she says hesitantly, "but it's still hard to have the responsibility of the bigger salary. Sometimes I think, *Why didn't I marry a guy who makes three hundred thousand dollars a year?* It's not like I want to have a closet full of Manolo Blahniks. I'd just like to have the luxury of feeling less pressured. I've also sacrificed time with my children because of the commute. There was something very comforting about knowing that in an emergency I could be with them within a few minutes when we lived closer to my office."

While changing the structure of your life by switching jobs, cutting your hours, or moving can often relieve some of the pressure, those options aren't realistic for many women who are their family's primary breadwinners. Others have found solace through subtler emotional means: a shift of perspective, say, or seeking out spiritual support.

When Andrea, fifty, married Paul, fifty-seven, nearly twenty years ago, he was a successful investment banker. "I don't think he ever slept through the night in the early days of our marriage," she says. "He worked so hard making sure all his deals were going well. As a result, he made very, very, very good money, and I had a lovely, carefree life—a beautiful home, two-week vacations to the Caribbean and Europe, the works."

They had two children within several years, and Paul wanted her "to stay home and be a mom." But she insisted on working a little, putting together fashion shows and corporate events for a number of different groups. "We were a two-income family, but my contribution was minuscule," she says. Five years after they were married, Paul was diagnosed with multiple sclerosis, and although he continued working, he had numerous setbacks. "The stress of his job exacerbated it," says Andrea.

Then, several years ago, a huge deal Paul was putting together went south, taking Paul's health along with it. The couple had to clean out their savings to stay solvent, and Andrea suddenly found herself with an invalid husband and a family of four to feed and clothe. "It was terrifying and exhilarating all at once," she says. "I had lots of contacts, and I just started calling people and making things happen. But I wouldn't have been able to get through it all if it weren't for my belief in God. That was the thing that held me together when I felt like I wanted to fall apart. I've always been a staunch Catholic, so when our lives started coming apart at the seams, I found a spiritual director—someone who could help me reassess my values and keep me focused on what's important. My spirituality is my grounding cord. When you lose all the material stuff, you need to visit the gifts you have inside, and for me it's my family and my talents. In some ways, I feel like my life really started to take off at age forty-nine."

Andrea is fortunate that she can seek spiritual solace. Fate has dealt her a hard blow. Although she undoubtedly experiences anger and frustration at Paul, his illness, and her situation as a whole, she doesn't blame him. Her religious beliefs help her to place her problems into a larger context, to realize that there are more profound issues at stake in the world, and to feel the support of her fellow parishioners. Going to church or synagogue—sharing religious, spiritual beliefs—strengthens the bonds in a marriage and within a family.

The women we spoke with who were happiest with their breadwinner status were those who went into it with their eyes wide open, knowing they'd always need to provide for their families and refusing to fall prey to fantasies of being rescued by a wealthy prince.

Brenda, forty-three, an interior designer who says she's comfortable with the fact that she makes more money than her husband, Charlie, fifty-two, an independent filmmaker, explains her attitude this way: "I met Charlie when I was thirty-four, and before that I had the typical *Sex in the City*, shitty noncommittal relationship after shitty noncommittal relationship. I dated tons of guys who made a lot of money, but they were such jerks I couldn't stand to be with them. Charlie was different. He's a great guy. Thoughtful and responsible. Now, don't get me wrong. I really do care about having money and nice things. I like to be pampered as much as the next person. But I think those bad experiences with men early on helped me change my priorities about who would make a good husband."

Even once they had a child, Brenda maintained her positive attitude about earning more than her husband. "Hey, I knew he didn't make much money when I met him. He is who he is. I never entertained the notion that he was going to be anyone else. I love what he does, and I believe in him. So what if I make more money? Our relationship works, because we both bring different things to the table, and that's fine with me."

Brenda and Charlie have a good thing going. Brenda brought a certain amount of life experience and maturity to her decision to marry Charlie. She valued him for his character and integrity, and by the time she married him she knew how vital that was in a long-term partnership. She respects him, believes in him, and admires him—behaviors that make him feel valued. She married him knowing what their arrangement would be, and she accepted her responsibilities. If she sometimes feels the need to be taken care of financially, she is able to put it aside. She obviously feels taken care of emotionally and psychologically by Charlie—she values the currency that he brought into the relationship—and that does make all the difference.

THE TIMES THEY ARE A-CHANGIN'

It's a bumpy ride for women today. Things are changing, and women are more independent and more powerful than ever before. There's still a long way to go, however, and we don't have all the answers yet. Our daughters and granddaughters will learn from what we accomplish and will have an easier time because we've paved the way.

As with all change, there can be some negative impact. Consider fifty-two-year-old Olivia's story. She told her parents when she was nine years old that she wanted to be a doctor. "They laughed," she recalls. "In those days, girls became nurses, not doctors. But I liked science and biology, and I thought, 'I'm not going to be a nurse. All girls are nurses. I'm going to be a doctor.'" True to her word, after college she went to medical school and became a dermatologist. That decision, she believes, "narrowed my choice of potential mates, because it takes a strong man to handle a woman with a 'masculine' career." As a result, she was delighted when she met Ethan, an occupational therapist, when she was in her early thirties.

"He wasn't intimidated by me or my career," she says. "At the time I thought it was because he got to know me in a personal situation, when I went to him for therapy." The couple married when she was thirty-four and, shortly thereafter, moved from the East Coast to Utah, where Olivia had been offered a job. It was then that Olivia began sensing that there might be a downside to her husband's ease with her financial dominance. "After we moved he was less than dogged in his pursuit of a new job," she says. "That should have tipped me off that there was a problem, but I didn't want to see it at the time."

By the time they moved again several years later, this time to Alabama, her salary was well into the six figures. "His lifestyle and expenditures went up accordingly," she says. "He bought a lot of toys—a fancy media system with surround sound, power tools, and heavy equipment like riding mowers. He had jobs off and on, but he seemed to lose interest in working, because he didn't really need to. We could live very comfortably on what I was making."

Despite the fact that she was troubled by Ethan's lack of ambition, the couple had two children within three years. Olivia soon realized, however, that Ethan wasn't going to be much help in raising them, either. "When I tried to share the responsibilities at home, things often went awry," she says. "If he was in charge of the kids, the three-year-old would end up wandering down the street. He just didn't pay attention to what was going on."

What eventually made the situation unbearable, she says, was his total lack of intellectual curiosity. "He never read a book or took a course or did anything really useful with his free time," she says. "It's one thing not to work. That's fine, I guess, if your spouse is making a lot of money. Plenty of women do that. But he didn't seem to want to do anything except hang out at the swimming pool."

After twelve years of marriage, she filed for divorce, she says, because she didn't have "an adult partner." "I was worried about the lessons I was teaching our two daughters about love and marriage," she says. "I didn't want them to think that marriage was a woman taking care of a man the whole time. I didn't want to be the one to show them what acquiescence is."

Who would have thought fifty years ago that the term *gold digger,* which still has an implicit female connotation, would be applicable to men? As more and more women with personal drive and earning power enter the marriage market, however, it's clear that what both sexes look for in a mate may begin to change.

In fact, there are hints that a shift is afoot already. While most studies show that men have always valued looks above all else in a potential spouse, researchers at Green Valley State University in Michigan uncovered a new trend. After analyzing the details of engagement announcements in a local newspaper over twenty-two years—they looked at couples' careers and educational attainment and even had a panel of students rate them based on their attractiveness—they concluded that in recent years men have started paying more attention to a potential spouse's education and earning potential than they have in the past.

Bob, thirty-four, isn't surprised. He says his wife Carla's intellect and ambition were more important to him than her looks. Now he works nights at a newspaper and stays home with their two children during the day while she goes to her job in a brokerage office. "When I was dating, I was definitely looking for someone in the professional world," he says. "I liked that Carla was educated and career-oriented. The fact that she makes good money wasn't as important, but it was a nice bonus."

In our dual-income world, where two salaries are increasingly necessary to meet the financial demands of a middle-class lifestyle, it's only logical that men will start looking for wives who can bring home a decent income. But as the financial responsibility among couples shifts, it has the potential to affect everything in the marriage, domino-like. In the upcoming chapters we'll explore the key areas of contention, from concrete issues like who does more housework to less tangible matters, like who holds decision-making power. Along the way we'll explain the most effective strategies for bringing old ideas about relationships and gender roles into the twenty-first century.

THREE

The Home Front

H ere's the typical scenario in our house," says Leigh, thirty-five. "When I come home from work I immediately shift into housewife mode—running around straightening things up, pulling food out of the refrigerator for dinner, going through the mail, listening to the messages. When Austin comes home from work he grabs the TV remote control and flops down on the couch, and he'll usually stay there unless I ask him to help me."

Her husband's attitude would be annoying in most dual-earner marriages, but in theirs it's truly preposterous, given that her salary as a commercial actress brings in about five times his income as a real estate broker. "It's not instinctive for him to clean up. He can walk right past a mess and not even notice—or maybe he notices, but he just figures I'll clean it up. In any case, I always have to ask him to help."

Trouble is, she hates asking. For one thing, she feels that Austin ought to be able to see what needs to be done as easily as she can. For another, she knows from bitter experience that sometimes when she does try to enlist his help, he accuses her of being a nag, a gender slur that has kept more than a few women quiet. But she's not the type to hold her tongue for long. "My mom was a homemaker, but my father was a really successful surgeon, and I identified more with his ambition and strength," she says. "I also inherited his way of dealing with people. That's not always a good thing. Let's just say I don't mince words."

When Austin is watching TV or reading the paper while she's cooking or cleaning, she says, she can feel the tension building and gaining momentum like an avalanche inside her. "I try to keep my frustration to myself and hope he'll notice how hard I'm working. But he usually doesn't, so I eventually get tired of it and just explode by saying something like 'What the hell do you think you're doing just sitting there?!!' "

Not surprisingly, her approach often backfires. Instead of engaging him in the household work, she succeeds only in engaging him in an argument, the same one they've had hundreds of times in the course of their seven-year marriage. "He says, 'I'm doing the best I can,' and I say, 'Well, it's not enough.' We never seem to get anywhere."

The unfairness she sees in the situation makes Leigh feel like her outbursts are fully justified. "I'm making way more money than he is," she says. "The least he could do is help around the house. I find it sort of unbelievable that I make most of the money *and* I pick up all the slack at home."

How did this vicious cycle start, and how will it ever end? Has housework become the stage for other, more painful, conflicts in the relationship? If Leigh really wants a change in Austin's behavior, then she needs a plan of attack that doesn't include angry accusations, which are clearly unproductive. Most men become very anxious and withdraw even further when their spouses get very angry at them. Women should certainly be able to express anger at their partners, bearing in mind that tone is key. If Leigh is waiting for Austin to feel sorry for her while she's sweating and fuming in the kitchen, then she will wait a good long time. Her suffering may make him feel guilty, but it will not make him do the dishes. Instead he will be angry at feeling manipulated and he will tune her out.

In the name of "working on the relationship," Leigh (and anyone in a similar position) needs to take the following steps: First, she must prepare Austin for a summit between them—a discussion that will take place several days or weeks down the road. She can do this in a playful or even flirtatious manner—whatever style works for her—as long as she's dead serious beneath the surface. Austin has to get used to the idea that an important conversation about their life together is imminent. Any woman who can orchestrate a serious conversation in the professional world has the tools to do this at home as well. When the time is right and they're both relaxed and enjoying each other's company, she needs to prep him for the summit. During this "prep" chat, she has to explain to Austin that she feels he is treating her unfairly and that it really hurts her feelings and even makes her think that he doesn't love her. If Austin laughs at her and brushes her off, she should say nothing more for the moment. This is difficult, but being patient at this stage will pay off later. It's important to not get angry (or, at the very least, to not show anger), because you want to set the stage for a levelheaded, mature discussion.

It may be necessary to repeat this prep step on several occasions, in a calm and good-natured manner. If Austin calls her a nag, she has to ignore it. It's just a ploy for him to avoid serious discussion.

She can also say that being a nag is not her intention. She could say something along the lines of "I love you and I'm trying to tell you how I feel."

After Leigh has laid the groundwork by alerting him to her hurt feelings and letting him know that she wants to have a serious discussion about it (all of which may take several weeks), she can schedule the summit and establish its format. They can agree that they will talk together for an hour at a certain time and place. They also should set some ground rules. Some that might be helpful: no walking out before the time is up; no raising voices; no interrupting while the other person is talking. Perhaps they can even take turns, each getting five minutes to talk, five minutes to listen.

The key for women in this position is to ask for what you want, no matter how hard it may be for you. Be specific. Men absolutely cannot read a woman's mind. You could write down a list of things that your husband can do to make you feel happy and loved by him, letting him know that these are just suggestions; everything is negotiable. In fact, you should encourage him to come up with some of his own ideas, which will help him feel more in control of the situation. You should let him know that you appreciate his cooperation—and constantly remind him and yourself that a relationship requires work. The work you're doing here is a positive and mature step toward a better marriage.

On the great invisible balance sheet of marriage, the fact that housework still falls squarely in the female column most of the time is enough to bring out the claws in even the most even-tempered, nonconfrontational women, much less in someone with a fiery temper like Leigh. Nowhere is the rift between the sexes more visible or the desire to cling to old gender roles more problematic than in this deeply fraught and fought-over realm.

Why are household tasks still such a sore spot in relationships?

Why don't men just step up to the plate and do their share around the house? Why do some women, who claim they want more help from their husbands, start nitpicking when men try to pitch in? And how can couples who have been raised to see housework as "her" work ever reach an egalitarian division of daily chores, or at least something that feels reasonable and fair? One summit at a time . . .

WE'VE COME A LONG WAY . . . MAYBE

Housework is not a new sore spot between men and women. In fact, it's such a common and well recognized problem that it's almost a cliché. But, as with most clichés, this one earned its status for a reason. Arlie Russell Hochschild dove headlong into the issue nearly fifteen years ago in her groundbreaking book *The Second Shift*, which examines the fact that working mothers have two jobs: the one they do from 9 A.M. to 5 P.M. (or, if current statistics are to be believed, to 6 or 7 P.M.) and the one they come home to, where a veritable assembly line of scut work—laundry, dishes, vacuuming, cooking—awaits. After interviewing fifty couples in depth, she concludes, "The majority of men did not share the load at home. Some refused outright. Others refused more passively, often offering a loving shoulder to lean on, an understanding ear as their working wife faced the conflict they both saw as hers."

Although a decade and a half has passed since Hochschild encouraged couples to open up about what goes on behind their closed doors, we found the same issues cropping up time and again in our interviews. There were, however, a few notable exceptions. Some of the stay-at-home dads we spoke with actually did the bulk of the drudge work, a role reversal that revealed true progress. Unfortunately, it, too, can have negative consequences, as we'll see later in this chapter, if women adopt the discriminatory attitudes of the patriarch breadwinners that went before them.

For the most part, women are still the de facto housekeepers even when they're also playing the primary-provider role. But let's give men some credit: As a group, they're better today than their fathers and grandfathers were about doing work around the house. Researchers in Maryland, who studied housework trends over the past thirty years, found that in 1965 women spent about thirty hours a week on chores while their husbands spent an average of 4.9 hours. By 1995, the playing field hadn't exactly been leveled, but the angle of the incline wasn't so steep: The hours women spent on housework had dropped to 17.5 a week, while men's had risen to 10. In 2004, the Department of Labor released a new survey that showed that almost as many women as men hold jobs (about 78 percent of women, compared with 85 percent of men) but that the average working woman spent about twice as much time as the average working man on household chores and the care of children.

The Maryland study found that two thirds of the time allotted to household tasks is spent on two main chores: cooking and cleaning. Men have made the most strides in the former. In fact, the idea of a man cooking is becoming downright trendy. Thanks to the proliferation of TV shows featuring male chefs like Emeril Lagasse, Rocco DiSpirito, and Jamie Oliver, many husbands are almost as at home in the kitchen as behind the barbecue grill, a traditional bastion of masculinity.

The Maryland researchers' data back this up. In 1965 women spent nearly nine times the number of hours in front of a stove as their mates, they found, but by 1995 men had taken up much of the slack. That's the glass-is-half-full perspective. Now for the half-empty view: Even with men's progress in the kitchen (arguably the most "fun" household task), women were still doing three times more cooking—hardly what you'd call a 50/50 split. And when you factor in other, less appealing, chores, like laundry, dishes, dusting, and vacuuming, on which women still spend up to seven times more hours than their husbands, the gender disparity around the house is even more bleak.

Underlying the hourly inequity is an attitude toward gender roles that seems to have stalled out somewhere around 1954, when men brought home all of the bacon and when it was expected that, in return, women would provide a peaceful, comforting, and loving home. Old beliefs die hard, even when the real world changes. Even among couples who appear to have overcome many of the ingrained beliefs about male and female roles and who share the household load more fairly, we found a surprising reluctance for men to take full ownership of the daily grind. Their attitude revealed itself in subtle ways. Some men we spoke with pointed out that they do more than their fathers did or that they're better about housework than many of their friends, as if they deserve a reward for doing anything at all. Others used phrases like "I pitch in" or "I help her out," comments that sound good on the surface but reveal a clear bias— that the ultimate responsibility for housework rests with their wives—lurking stubbornly underneath. One telling study found that men who support feminist ideas only do an average of four minutes more housework a day than traditional men—a finding that reveals how difficult it can be to jettison old ideas about who should be doing what.

Why are men so disinclined to change with the times? Hochschild theorized that, when a wife brings home a paycheck, men start feeling their male power ebbing, like Superman when he's exposed to kryptonite. As a result, they try to restore their rightful place at the family helm by refusing to participate in so-called women's work. She explains, "According to this principle, if men lose power over women in one way, they make up for it in another way—by avoiding the second shift, for example. In this way, they can maintain dominance over women. How much responsibility these men assumed at home was thus related to the deeper issue of male power."

Lots of the men we talked to had a much more superficial explanation. "She cares more than I do if the house is neat," explains Barry, a playwright. "I would eventually get around to doing my dishes, washing the laundry, emptying the trash. But Anne always gets to it before me." Barry and Anne's situation is far from unique.

Women are also culpable in the war over who does what at home, because many won't ask for help. It definitely takes two to tango. Because women also are in the midst of a confusing revolution in family life, they aren't really sure what's right themselves. That makes it hard for them to ask for anything. They may be the primary family breadwinner, but their heads are back in 1954 (really not so long ago, when you think about it) and down deep they believe that they are and should be the family caretaker. But when asked point-blank how they feel about their household inequities, we found the majority are secretly seething. Those long-suffering souls who uncomplainingly pull the second shift—changing out of their shiny suits of armor when they get home from work and into the grubby sweatpants that speak volumes about their household roles—may actually harbor more resentment than their more outspoken sisters. They stay silent to preserve the peace in their marriages or, as Hochschild theorizes, to protect their lower-earning husbands' egos. "Sensing their husbands got 'touchy,' sensing the fragility of their husbands' 'male ego,' not wanting them to get discouraged or depressed, such women restored their men's lost power by waiting on them at home," she writes.

Those feelings of resentment and anger don't just magically disappear, no matter how much we try to will them away. They resurface in other ways and other places, including the bedroom, as we'll see in chapter 5, inevitably increasing, rather than decreasing, the tension and antipathy in the marriage. Conversely, studies show that when men carry their fair share of the housework (which doesn't necessarily mean half, by the way, but rather an amount that feels equitable to both partners) women have significantly lower heart rates during marital spats—a sign that they are calm and, as a result, more likely to be able to broach any conflict in a productive, non-confrontational manner.

What will become clear as you read the couples' stories in this chapter is that for most people housework isn't just housework. For men it has everything to do with masculinity, power, pride, and shame. For women, it's about a complex, combustible mix of femininity, control, and the deep desire to have their contributions recognized and appreciated. The interaction of men's and women's often conflicting needs and desires can fuel many painful arguments.

YOU SAY POTATO, HE HEARS POTAHTO

"David never, ever, does enough around the house, in my opinion," says Caroline, the market-research analyst we met in the introduction. She not only earns far more than he but also is home far less, because he's self-employed and has an office in their house. And yet, to her utter exasperation, she still does more of the household chores. "He's very good about the kid stuff," she continues, "and he does the laundry, which is a big help. But it would never occur to him to empty the dishwasher or even take down the Christmas tree. There could be mounds of refuse lying around, and he wouldn't see it."

As frustrated as she gets, she's learned she has to tread very lightly when she raises the issue. "He assumes that any criticism from me is only a veiled way of saying that I'm disappointed he doesn't make more money," she says. "It all comes back to that for him. When I tell him I need more help, he hears that he's not making enough money. He's convinced that I secretly wish he were still an investment banker, but I really don't. I just wish he'd make dinner more often or scrub the kitchen floor."

It's a little hard to ask a former investment banker who can't seem to find similar work to feel happy about scrubbing a floor. Of course, a woman in the same situation would not feel mopping as such a blow to her pride, because she would be used to the idea that that's what women do. In the past, women did the dirty work at home and never got much praise for it. But what we all need to realize is that nobody, man or woman, enjoys mopping floors. Housework is drudgery. It's not supposed to be fun (except for those who really get a kick out of being neat). But it's something that we need to do in order to keep the family corporation functioning. Being married doesn't guarantee happiness 100 percent of the time. Being married means being married. And that takes work of all kinds.

Caroline needs to let David know how much she appreciates everything he's doing for the family, and clearly he's doing quite a bit. She also needs to be truthful and open—to spell out for him that if she asks him to do something he doesn't want to do, it's not because she's rubbing his face in the mud. She is asking for help because she really needs it. And she also has to admit (and here she has to keep her guilt in check) that she is asking him to do a grungy job that she dislikes doing herself.

Underneath the misinterpretations and misunderstandings about housework lies the shame David feels about his wife outearning him.

A quiet, unprepossessing guy raised in a traditional family, he can feel emasculated by their situation—a feeling that may be heightened by the fact that Caroline herself has a powerhouse personality. With undergrad and graduate degrees from an Ivy League university and enough enthusiasm and energy for half a dozen women, she could make even the strongest man feel a bit intimidated.

"I'm up at four forty-five every morning to exercise, and I leave for work at six forty-five," says Caroline. "I'm a very hard worker, and I have a lot of energy. I really value those traits in people, and David knows that. But what he doesn't see is that his job doesn't have to come with a big paycheck for me to respect it. As long as he works hard and accomplishes things, I'll be happy. If his passion was dog grooming but he was hands down the best dog groomer, I'd be thrilled." Early in their relationship, when David was outearning Caroline five or six times over, he undoubtedly felt that his financial clout balanced her personal chutzpa. But now that she's the primary breadwinner, that balance has shifted, and it's difficult for him to find other ways to assert himself, at least ways that don't feel feminine, soft, or embarrassingly second-rate.

Because she knows how sensitive he is, Caroline tries not to criticize David every time she comes home to a jam-encrusted countertop. When she feels the fatigue and weight of her financial responsibility bearing down, she reminds herself of the other contributions he makes to their marriage—particularly in the realm of child care—that give her the freedom to stay at work until 8 or 9 P.M. if she needs to. "He drops our son off at school and picks him up, takes him to karate and Little League, and bears down on the nightly homework," says Caroline. "When I come home, I get to play with him rather than be the homework heavy, and for that I am everlastingly grateful and relieved."

Caroline gets a lot of support from David, and she knows it. But it's not enough for her that David lightens her load, and it may never be. She seems very sensitive to David's feelings of insecurity about his masculinity, and her sensitivity to his situation can only help to cement their relationship. She's right to ignore jam-encrusted countertops—in the larger scheme of things there are far worse offenses than sticky counters. And in situations like Caroline's, women must learn to accept the fact that their homes are not going to be perfectly neat and clean and orderly. If she wants more help from David, then she has to be very specific in asking for it. But what's probably more important for Caroline than getting David to wipe the counter is learning to let go of her need for order and accepting that her home will never be as clean and well organized as her mother's.

Men like David (most men, in fact) have internalized the message of their fathers—that real men provide for their families. Many of them never saw their fathers lift a finger around the house and probably didn't receive much encouragement from them to do so, either. In times past, men's breadwinning responsibilities served as a handy rationalization (unfair though it may be) for them to bow out of the daily household grind. But in many couples today, that patriarch mentality is no longer justifiable through economics. Even so, its influence lingers and may even be exacerbated by the fact that the wife brings home the bacon.

In Hochschild's interviews, she found that of the men who earned more than their wives, 21 percent shared household work. In couples who brought home equal-sized paychecks, about 30 percent of the men shared the burden at home. But among men who earned less than their wives, exactly none participated in the second shift.

Our interviews show that men's attitudes have evolved over the past decade or so. Most of the men we spoke with haven't reacted to their wives' larger paychecks by totally loafing at home. But they still struggle with striking what their wives would consider a fair balance—and until they accept the fact that housework is work that both partners share, the issue will continue to cause them grief, to frustrate their working wives, and to ignite conflict in their relationships.

NEUTERING THE NOTION
OF HOUSEWORK

"Before we had kids we had endless battles over the fact that I did more around the house than Mason," says Rose, forty-one, a screenwriter, who supported Mason, forty-two, through business school and has continued to do so as he pursues his dream of helping disadvantaged youth. "It irritated me that I did more of the cooking and cleaning, but I guess I always sort of expected to do that. What really made me mad, though, is that he didn't do any of the traditional male stuff around the house, either. I did all the handyman work myself, or else I hired someone to do it. He wouldn't even change a lightbulb! If one burned out, it would just stay that way until I changed it."

Most of the couples we interviewed made the distinction between "guy things" (which usually consist of yard work, cleaning the garage or basement, taking out the trash, and maintaining the cars) and "women's work"—essentially the inside chores—as if there were some invisible, unbroachable line separating the two spheres. And many wives accepted their husbands' "guy work" as a fair and equal contribution to the family chores. But on closer examination, we realized that the "his work/her work" divide actually contributes to women's feelings of frustration, because often the male sphere is in no way comparable to the female one. One study asked women and men to list their household chores and found that their lists contained roughly the same number of items. But the seeming equity is deceptive, because men's tasks—"mow the lawn," "take out the trash"—are jobs that are done once a week or once a month ("wash the car"), whereas women's chores are distinguished by their relentless dailiness.

Most high-earning wives know this separate-but-unequal concept all too well, whether they acknowledge it openly in their relationships or not. "Laundry is the bane of my existence," says Claire, a harried breadwinning mother who doesn't have any household help. "Every day my kids dirty at least one outfit and often two or three. I sometimes imagine them walking around the house yelling for me, only to find me days later buried under a mound of dirty clothes. It's an endless, thankless job. Greg will mow the lawn once every week or so and act like he's evened the score, but that doesn't even come close."

What's at issue in the "male work" versus "female work" debate is time and energy and who is expending more of those two scarce commodities. As a result, it can be revealing to bring the subject out of the laundry room, as it were, and into the open. To get an objective sense of who does what, each partner should make a list of the chores he or she does, along with how often they need to be performed and how much time they take. If there's an unfair discrepancy in the totals, don't assume that a lightbulb will go off for the partner who's doing less. Men do not have revelations when it comes to housework. The discrepancy has to be pointed out to them, even if it makes them squirm. Unfortunately, suggestions or requests are often taken as criticism by men who feel that they are not being appreciated for everything they do contribute—and often they're right. So be sure to acknowledge that you appreciate their efforts even if, like so many overburdened women, you have little patience for men who feel overburdened as well.

Another advantage of listing your chores is that when they're in black and white they tend to be desexualized. Men may perceive vacuuming or doing the dishes as female, but when the words are written alongside other tasks like "take out the garbage" it can help them see that there is nothing innately feminine or masculine about any of it—it's just work that needs to be done to keep the household running properly.

It may also help women to explain to their husbands the benefits of a more even division of labor. This would again require a "summit meeting." (See the beginning of this chapter for more detailed instructions on staging a major discussion.) In the summit, first and foremost you need to establish that you're genuinely at the end of your rope. Men may not believe this readily, since many of their mothers have spoiled them. Generally, unless their spouse becomes extremely ill or otherwise disabled, men don't consider household messes *their* problem.

Next, you have to tell your husband calmly, quietly, and earnestly that he cannot continue to function the way he has been— that there is an imminent danger of breakdown in the operations of the household. Right-brained creatures that they are, men do better with concrete information than with innuendo or hints. So spell it out: "I'll have more energy at the end of the day for other activities (wink, wink) if I don't have so much to do around the house." Or "We're both so much happier when the house is clean, and it will be clean more often if we both make more of an effort to tidy up." Keep in mind that the way you ask for things—your tone of voice and your language—can make a big difference in the way your husband responds. Tact and diplomacy are important in any negotiation. An aggressive approach almost never works, while a neutral, loving, or playful one often does.

Claire used this strategy to great success. Early on in their marriage, she says, she had a greater need for household order than Greg did. "I explained in a jokey tone that I wasn't trying to be a shrew, that it really helped my peace of mind to walk into a clean house. I also hinted that at the end of the day I'd have much more energy left for romance if he'd help me out. Once we had kids, he started to get it more. Now, when there are clothes all over the floor and toys covering the kitchen counter, it makes him as buggy as it does me. We'll look at each other and say, 'The walls are starting to close in. It's time to fight back.' And we'll spend a whole day getting things organized again."

Here's the strategy that helped Rose finally get Mason to do more of the work around the house. "After we had our first child I could feel myself cracking under the pressure of all my responsibility," she says, "so I went to Mason and very calmly listed all the things I do. Then I let him pick which ones he wanted to take on. He now does the laundry and the grocery shopping and pays the bills. It's made my life a million times easier. I still do more around the house. But I don't feel so resentful, because I can see he's making a contribution. He lightened my load, which is really all I was asking for."

DEALING WITH HOUSEWORK DUDS

Although there are undoubtedly men who tend more toward the Felix Unger end of the neatness spectrum, we're probably not in danger of stereotyping when we say that many men lean more toward the Oscar Madison style of housekeeping. "The slob gene definitely seems more common in men," says Claire. "I don't know a single woman who has a husband who is neater than she is, but I've heard they exist."

Claire says that although Greg has gotten better about many chores, she despairs of ever getting him to help when it comes to tackling their family's endless piles of laundry. In theory, he's willing to help, she says; but in practice his help is sometimes more of a hindrance. "He lets it pile up for so long that the kids run out of clean underwear, or he'll do some lamebrained thing like wash eight loads in fabric softener instead of detergent. I sometimes wonder if he's really incapable of doing the job or he just pretends to be so he can weasel his way out of helping."

Men's unfamiliarity with housework, with exactly how much effort it takes to get the toothpaste splatters off the bathroom mirror or the red-wine stain out of the living room carpet, often comes off as a bumbling ineptness that may reflect not only their lack of childhood role models but also their disinterest in becoming proficient housekeepers. Why learn to clean the shower grout or swipe the cobwebs out of the corners if you think that by doing it poorly you stand a better chance of losing the unpleasant job for good? What's more, like Barry, the playwright, they may not even notice or be bothered by the toothpaste splatters in the first place.

Women who like order, like Claire, and Barry's wife, Anne, can't possibly let the laundry or the dishes pile up until their husbands finally notice and jump in. Male slobs will *never* jump in. But if these women would actually let the laundry and dishes pile up, they would have a better chance in negotiations during a summit. This is much easier to do before children enter the picture. If you realize before children arrive that you have married an incorrigible slob, then you must retrain him. He has not been brought up well in terms of being prepared to live with a woman other than his mother. During the retraining phase it's important that you don't do any of his laundry or put anything of his away. W. Bruce Cameron, in his book *How to Remodel a Man,* suggests that you try hiding TV remotes or other things that are important to him in his piles and when he is looking for them, just shrug and tell him "it must have disappeared in all of your stuff." It may take some time, so steel yourself—but eventually, he will clean up his act.

Once you have children, the retraining becomes more complicated as you are forced to prioritize the areas in which you want your husband's cooperation. Many couples credit housekeepers with saving their marriages. If you can possibly afford it, consider making that investment. Even if you can swing it once every two weeks or monthly, so that someone else can do the floors, bathrooms, and heavy lifting, it's a pretty obvious way to ease your load and bring some peace (and cleanliness) into the home.

When they're pushed to perform, many men prove—to themselves and their eternally grateful wives—that a Y chromosome doesn't doom a person to household incompetence. "In the early days when he was at home, Timothy never did anything—no laundry, no cooking, no dishes," says Lisa, whose husband, a former trader we mentioned in chapter 1, is now a stay-at-home dad. "But it's evolved over time. I think he sees that life is much nicer—the kids are calmer, the house feels more peaceful—when things aren't in such a terrible state of disarray."

Austin Murphy, a sportswriter, took a six-month sabbatical from his job at *Sports Illustrated* to tackle the job of full-time dad while his wife, Laura, plunged into her own career as a writer. In his humorous book about the experience, *How Tough Could It Be?* he sums up his learning curve: "I am now equipped to be a bigger help for the remainder of our days together. When I'm home, I'm cooking a couple of nights a week. I'm grocery shopping, laundry folding, floor sweeping—you name it . . . Sure there remains a gap in our standards, so that I will always be doing less than I think I am doing. But every little bit helps. If I am not, like Thomas, a 'very useful engine,' I am at least a more useful engine than I was. For now, that will have to do."

Even men who have risen to the occasion and accepted that housework is a part of their newfound identities may exhibit certain peculiarly male characteristics, however—they want credit for everything they do around the house, say, or they exaggerate their contributions. Clay, the stay-at-home dad who plays poker on the side, says he and his wife, Sarah, split the cleaning 50/50, but she begs to differ. "He does the dishes, takes out the garbage and recycling, and grocery shops, but I'm the one who does most of the day-to-day cleaning and straightening," she says. "I sometimes don't think he realizes how much I do." Rather than harboring resentment, Sarah might be better off enlisting Clay's help. She could say, "Why don't you vacuum while I clean the kitchen so we'll have time to go to a movie later?" This sort of teamwork approach often appeals to the male sensibility, as will the idea that the reward for pitching in is more couple time.

Men need to feel appreciated as much as women do. But since we are in the midst of a social revolution with many stops and starts and turbulence all the way round, we're not very good at expressing appreciation for each other. The middle of a social revolution is not the best time for power plays or ego wrestling, though. Rather, this is a time to remind each other that things are tough, that you need compassion for each other, that you're both pioneers, and that you are committed to finding solutions and making them work.

LETTING GO OF YOUR NEED
FOR CONTROL

On the flip side, many men complain that their wives are overly picky and demanding, that when they *do* try to help around the house, their wives say they don't do the chores "right." They raise a valid point. If men need to help out more, then women need to be willing to relinquish control over how things are done—how the dishwasher is loaded, how the laundry is folded, how spotless the bathroom is. Let's face it: No one likes to feel like his every effort is being scrutinized and criticized, and the white-glove approach can backfire, by making men more resentful than they need to be. For some women, however, letting their husbands do things their way is more difficult than it sounds.

"I'm pretty particular when it comes to housework," admits Leigh. "My attitude is: If you're going to do it, do it right. When I try to tell Austin how to fold sheets, for instance, he storms off in a huff. I wouldn't get mad if he tried to tell me how to put oil in the car. I just don't understand why he can't accept my help around the house." Anne, who runs her own business, has similar issues with delegating. "If Barry goes to the supermarket, he will inevitably buy horrible-colored cereal for the kids, and stuff that we already have. He doesn't do shopping lists. And it would never occur to him to pick up something as basic as milk, which we always need."

In some cases—if the toilet looks as dirty after he cleans it as before or the clean laundry sits in a basket for three weeks before he puts it away—a criticism of your husband's efforts may be valid, and it's important to be able to point out the problem. But pick and choose what you point to, otherwise you will, after all, become a nag.

In other cases—you think he should use a sponge to clean under the toilet rim, but he prefers using the toilet brush—a desire to intercede may indicate an inability to give up control of household chores, a sign of women's conflicted relationship with housework. While we don't want to be the family slave, as Katherine said in the introduction, we may cling to gender-specific activities like cleaning to reassure ourselves and our mates that underneath the successful façade (and the big paycheck) we're really still essentially "feminine."

Household chores feel comfortingly familiar to many women, who watched their mothers and grandmothers perform similar tasks for their families. When we're cooking and cleaning for our husbands, we're on safe territory, taking care of our men the way women have for decades, being good girls, and listening to the internalized voices of our mothers, not rejecting them or the lifestyles they chose. The money we make gives us a freedom and power our mothers never had in relation to the men in their lives. Yet we know that we owe our mothers a great debt, and the idea of rejecting their lives out of hand makes us uneasy. When we're out in the work world our conflicts about this make us feel that we are less socially acceptable, less nurturing, and therefore less female—even less good. There's a lot going on inside us that chips away at our self-esteem and self-confidence.

Many women report feeling a sense of order when their house is clean and tidy—and a sense of anxiety when it is not. This is not only childhood training. This need for household order reflects our need to order all of the confusing feelings and conflicts within us, projected onto the outside world. It's our attempt to do two things at once—work and nurture—and to do both equally well. Women experience a terrible inner tug-of-war, and it can tear them apart if they aren't careful. They have to relinquish the need for complete control of their households, which is not easy.

EVERYONE WANTS TO BE
APPRECIATED

For women who make more money than their husbands, their spouse's lack of participation around the house is the ultimate blow, a sign that he doesn't respect or appreciate how hard she works during her day job, much less her financial contribution to the family. It can be indicative of the fact that, while he pays lip service to their equality, deep down he still sees his leisure time as more important than hers.

Danika, twenty-eight, a freelance proofreader, puts it this way: "I do more around the house, but I don't see any way to make it fifty/fifty right now, because I work at home and Matt, my husband, doesn't. What bothers me more is the fact that he doesn't seem to notice when I buy the groceries or walk the dog. He certainly doesn't seem grateful for it if he does notice. But those things all take time and effort."

Danika says that Matt's lack of perspective on her workload became clear to her several months ago when they were having a discussion about how she could find more time for her career. "Between taking care of our new baby and doing all the daily household chores," she says, "I was having a hard time seeing how I was going to get any work done, and that, of course, would be very bad for the family seeing as I make about half again as much as Matt does. I said to him, 'I guess I'll just have to get up at five A.M., and he just sort of said, 'Yeah, maybe,' in this sympathetic voice. That pissed me off. He doesn't get the kind of effort I'm putting into our lives. He would never get up that early to work, yet he takes for granted that I would."

Although Danika's feelings are understandable, her approach to the issue was less than helpful, because she was expecting Matt to in-tuit what she needed instead of telling him outright. Rather than re-sorting to sarcasm, she should have told Mike outright that she was feeling overwhelmed and needed help. One of the biggest mistakes women make on the household battleground is expecting men to notice what they've done around the house—and then feeling hurt and unappreciated when they don't.

When a woman makes more money than her husband, she wants her contribution to be acknowledged; she wants the marital credit column to reflect the weight of her daily responsibility; she wants the respect she feels is a provider's due—the respect that gen-eration after generation of male providers before her have received. In *The Second Shift*, Arlie Russell Hochschild calls this phenomenon "the economy of gratitude," which she explains this way: "When couples struggle, it is seldom simply over who does what. Far more often, it is over the giving and receiving of gratitude." But that credit and appreciation is the very thing that some men, particularly the ones who are struggling emotionally with the financial disparity, are reluctant to give.

"I'm sometimes stunned at how ungrateful Austin seems," says Leigh. "It makes me want to hit him over the head and say, 'You don't know how good you have it.' I make tons of money so we can have this nice life and take nice vacations and afford a nanny. Sure, he works hard at his job. But his financial contribution is so much less than mine I guess I expect a little recognition of that fact now and again."

Learning to acknowledge the contributions your husband makes, and helping him see the value of your work, both inside and outside the home, will help you transcend the petty world of "his" work or "her" work and help you both become partners in the truest sense of the word. It's worth investing some time and psychic energy to try to get there. Research has shown that people who believe their close relationships are fairly equitable are more satisfied than those who see big inequities. But more recent studies have found that people who don't buy into traditional gender stereotypes—a trait that often characterizes high-achieving women—have an even greater expectation of equity in their relationships than those who have a more traditional point of view. They want to believe that their husbands are working as hard as they are at whatever they are doing, and they want to feel an essential "fairness" in the situation. This issue is likely to take an ever greater toll in the marriages of female breadwinners unless it is confronted head-on—brought out into the open and carefully considered and discussed.

Equity doesn't necessarily mean a rigid 50/50 split of household chores, however, and appreciation doesn't have to come in the form of a verbal thank-you. Danika, for instance, says, "Matt can be really thoughtful sometimes. When a group of friends were going hiking on the first nice day recently, he suggested I go while he stayed home with the baby. Now, I know he would have loved to have gone on that hike, but he put my needs ahead of his. I think that's his way of saying thank you, rather than coming right out and saying it." She adds thoughtfully, "If I wanted to, I could get pretty bent out of shape about being the grocery shopper and the child caretaker, but it's not worth it. There are days when I'm frustrated, but ninety-five percent of the time I'm pretty psyched. In most ways Matt is a great husband. What he lacks in household cleanliness he makes up for with emotional support. All in all, we have a happy life." It would go a long way if Danika expressed her appreciation of Matt's gesture and would probably lead to other thoughtful gestures. Once again, men need love and appreciation as much as women do.

Some stay-at-home dads have the same complaints about their wives' lax attitudes toward housework as their female predecessors of yesteryear. "My wife has attempted to clean one bathroom in the seventeen years we've been together," says Steve, whom we profiled in chapter 1. "I've always had all the responsibility for the household chores, even when I was working outside the house, mostly because I've always been much neater than Kimberly. We have two kids now and a big house—about four thousand square feet—so I've had to tone down my cleaning a bit. I tell myself that everything doesn't have to be spic-and-span every second of the day. It's hard for me, though, and it can be very frustrating when Kimberly comes home and throws her stuff around. It feels like a real slap in the face—like what I do isn't important."

WHEN HE IS THE NEATNIK

Although most stay-at-home dads we spoke with say their bread-winner wives also share the household responsibility, the men who carried the burden alone felt as disrespected and unappreciated as traditional housewives of thirty years ago. But women today should know better. Having seen their mothers and grandmothers oppressed for years, they should realize that it makes no sense to become the oppressor when the opportunity arises. It's muddled thinking. Women need to pull themselves together and ask themselves what on earth they expect to accomplish with a contemptuous attitude. Contempt is a surefire way to destroy a marriage.

Sharon had been less than appreciative of her stay-at-home husband Scott's contributions around the house. She recalls guiltily, "I actually said to him one day, 'I'm out there slaying dragons to keep our family going, and you can't even fucking buy skim milk!' We had many arguments, because I never felt like he was doing enough around the house or doing chores the right way. When I criticized him, he'd say, 'Stop treating me like an employee,' and I'd fire right back by saying, 'Stop treating me like an ATM.' "

Sharon and Scott started seeing a therapist, which helped them recognize and appreciate each other's contributions to the family. But the thing that really opened Sharon's eyes was spending three months on bed rest when she was pregnant with their second child. "I had the chance to see how much he did during the day. He never stopped moving. Between trying to take care of our toddler and keep the house picked up, he had his hands really full. It was the first time it struck me that his job is actually harder than mine."

COUPLES WHO MAKE IT WORK

For couples in which women make more money than their husbands, it's rare that housework is a nonissue. Even those who have regular housekeeping help still bicker about the small messes we all create on a daily (sometimes hourly!) basis. But wives and husbands who are able to talk about the issue and negotiate (and renegotiate) a fair distribution of work are way ahead of the game.

Sandy, fifty-three, a magazine editor, and Ben, fifty-seven, have been married twenty years. Theirs is a mixed union, both religiously and politically. "He's Catholic, I'm Jewish," she says. "He's conservative, I'm liberal. We fought so much early on in our relationship that I always say we had our divorce before we got married." The net result of their early wrangling has been positive, however. "In hindsight, I can see that our early differences were helpful, because we both understood from the beginning that there were no assumptions about anything. From the start we knew that everything got talked about."

They made about the same amount of money when they met, but when Ben quit his job twelve years ago to pursue his dream of being a sculptor, they immediately discussed the ramifications his move would have on their relationship—as well as on who did what at home. "We both understood that his contribution wasn't going to be financial," Sandy says, "so we agreed that he would be mostly responsible for the house—for the laundry and the cleaning. It's worked out fairly well. It's not like I come home to dinner on the table and a shiny, clean house every day. But then again, if I were the one at home, it wouldn't be that way, either. I felt fortunate to have a parent in the house when our two children were young."

Ben agrees that the situation has worked well. "I found it intensely pleasurable to be home with the kids, and if that meant taking on the majority of the household chores, so be it. I am an interior person, and sculpting is what I love to do. I really enjoy the solitude and the process of creating something. I appreciated the fact that this was a great opportunity for me, and I've always been grateful to Sandy for being willing to take on the financial responsibility."

Johnny, who stays at home with three children (we introduced him in chapter 1), says that housekeeping comes naturally to him. "My mom has a master's degree in home economics, and she really shaped my upbringing," he says. "I was taught at an early age how to do my own laundry and how to cook and sew. I'm very task-oriented, so housework suits my personality. I think a lot of guys would like it if they could get over the idea that it's 'women's work.'" In addition to the housework, he does the yard work, the laundry, and the bills. "If one of the kids wakes up in the middle of the night, I consider it my responsibility, because Jill works," he says.

Even so, they've had to work out some sticking points and be respectful of each other's point of view. "If Jill says something about the house not being clean, I say, 'I'll keep the house clean when you keep your closet clean.' Her closet has always been her responsibility—and it's usually a mess." Jill says she's learned to accept a less-than-pristine house by acknowledging that, on the whole, their situation works well. "He's no June Cleaver," she says, "but I'm not either. I have my moments when I want to say, "Geez, you could have done the laundry . . . but he takes care of all our bills and runs all the errands and does sweet extra things like making sure there's gas in my car. I can't complain, really.'"

She also decided to hire a housekeeper to come every two weeks to do the serious deep cleaning that was hard for Johnny to get to. Again, for families who have the resources, hiring some help—even once a month—can go a long way toward keeping domestic battles at bay. But even couples who do all the work themselves can do so peacefully. Allen and Alicia, whom we wrote about in chapter 1, divide chores "not along gender lines but by who has the time and resources to do what," Allen says. "Because I'm home until two or three P.M., I do the laundry, make the bed, clean the kitchen, and take the dog for a walk. She usually cooks dinner because she gets home from work between four and five P.M., and she'll do things like vacuum and dust. It works out well. We see ourselves as a team. When we both pitch in the load is so much lighter."

To put it simply, it's important for the health and happiness of your marriage for both of you to accept the fact that housework isn't just a woman's job. Husbands who help aren't simply easing their wife's burden; they're doing the necessary work to make the marriage and the family function more efficiently. Wives who enlist their husband's help and appreciate his efforts will see an upward spiral in marital happiness and a greater commitment from their spouse to the daily chores. The same principles hold true when it comes to child care, the focus of the next chapter, but the issues that come up—and the intensity of the emotions that accompany them—can catch many contemporary couples by surprise.

FOUR

Bringing Up Baby

espite the fact that I work long hours, I've always been the commander in chief at home," says Leah, the litigator we wrote about in chapter 2 who feels trapped by her New York City career and lifestyle. "I've been responsible for everything from the pencils our daughters need at preschool to their emotional well-being—and that has made me very happy." She and Frank have been married for eight years, and she's always been the main family breadwinner, a position she held gladly until last year, when Frank left his job in corporate communications to stay home full-time with their two young daughters.

"Something in me snapped when Frank became a stay-at-home dad," she says. "I felt like my relationship with my daughters would be marginalized by him being with them more than I am. I actually sat at work one day and figured out how many extra hours he'd be spending with them every year while I'm at work. I was worried that the girls and I would lose our closeness and, to be perfectly honest, that I'd lose the sense of control I've always had over their lives and well-being. When I'm sixty, I don't want my kids to say, 'Mom worked her butt off and Daddy made the lunches.' "

Intellectually, Leah knows it's better to have their children with her husband than with a nanny, but emotionally the idea is still "like a dagger in the heart," she says. "I sometimes say to myself, 'Just grow up. This is a good situation. Focus on the positive.' But then one of the girls will run to Frank when she falls down, and it just kills me. I'm ridiculously sensitive to those things right now. I never would have thought this before I had children, but I really believe there's some special bond between mothers and their kids. I work almost exclusively with men, and I don't see any of them worrying that their wives get to spend more time with their children. They're not calculating the number of hours they're missing at home."

She sighs, then adds, "Frank asked me the other day if I'm angry at him, and the truth is, I'm not. I can't blame him for not being a breadwinner, because I knew he wasn't going to be one when I met him. I'm angry at life. I guess I could be angry that I made some of the choices I made, but how could I have known when I was going to law school how I'd feel once I had kids? It's impossible to know that when you're young and single. If I really wanted to, I could quit my job and demand that we move to Boise. But I'm forty-eight, and I worry about making a career change at this stage in life. I need to provide financial security for the girls as they get older. The arrangement we have right now—me working long hours, Frank staying home—doesn't feel acceptable to me, and yet I don't have any idea what to do about it."

Many women like Leah experience agony over the physical separation from their children and any possible disruption of the close emotional maternal bond. Mothering their children unconsciously brings women back to blissful childhood feelings of oneness with their own mother—an experience they yearn to replicate with their own children. This intense need for the emotional bond with their children often evokes jealousy of their husbands or their nannies. Men also feel the need for this closeness, but they have learned early on to separate from their mother, so they unconsciously protect themselves from the intensity of these longings.

Leah doesn't see men at work worrying about their wives spending more time with their children because working men feel that they are being good fathers when they're providing the money to help support the family. They are generally more comfortable with the idea of someone else caring for their children. It's hard to know from our present vantage point, in the midst of this turbulent evolution in family life, if women will ever feel satisfied in the same way. Although it's unlikely, one bonus for breadwinning mothers is that they have more control than nonworking mothers over financial decisions regarding their children—they're earning more money, so they usually have at least an equal say (sometimes more) in how it's spent. Although they will usually consult with their husbands, they really don't need permission to spend.

Of course, when women like Leah feel resentful of their husband's relationship with their children, they put their husbands in an impossible situation, which Leah acknowledges. What on earth is Frank to do about her feelings? He's damned if he does and damned if he doesn't. Leah needs to tell Frank that despite her jealousy, she wouldn't want him to be any less of a wonderful parent than he is, that she loves him for it and that she would never want it any other way. If she does, he'll be better able to accept her turbulent emotions for what they are: a sign of the confusion that many breadwinning wives quite naturally experience. Neither Leah nor

Frank have real role models for their cutting-edge arrangement. Because they are on their own, they need to turn to each other to share their feelings, talk things over, and find solutions that feel comfortable to both of them.

Many aspects of women's lives have changed in the past forty years, since Betty Friedan's call for housewives to throw off the shackles of gender bias and fulfill themselves in other ways—intellectually, creatively, professionally. We've heeded that call, proving ourselves capable in the workplace—virtually any workplace. Gaining entrance to the professional world has been a boon for women, emotionally as well as financially, and yet, when we have children many of us start to feel a deep rift forming at the center of our lives. It's as if we're being pulled in two directions. On the one hand, we have a pressing desire to continue reaping the emotional and financial rewards of our chosen careers, to challenge our intellects and plumb the far reaches of our individual talents. On the other is the ancient tug to nurture children, to care for them, to spend not just quality time but quantity time with them—to be mothers, complete with all the minute-by-minute joys and frustrations that entails. The emotional tug-of-war is enough to make even some of the most committed professionals, like Leah, reexamine their values and priorities.

A number of the women we spoke with were less inclined to see kids as an impediment to their careers than to see their professional demands as an obstacle to spending time with their children. While most don't want to (or can't) give up their hard-won professional achievements, neither do they want to look back in fifty years with a bank account full of money and a heart filled with regret.

THE LAST TABOO:
MATERNAL LONGING

"I found that whenever I was out of the house for more than a couple of hours a day, I felt an invisible tether drawing me home," writes clinical psychologist Daphne de Marneffe, Ph.D., in her book *Maternal Desire*. "I couldn't bear to leave our baby; when I was away, I ached, and in her presence, I couldn't imagine a worthwhile reason for leaving her. And, rather than being a feeling I wanted to diminish or overcome, it was one I wanted to endorse and embrace." Later on she adds, "I was the site of colliding motives; my wish to care for my child was something I felt both hesitant to admit and called to defend, and the conflict made it hard to utter anything genuine at all."

It's shocking that women have to defend a normal longing to be with their babies. Despite the extraordinary changes we are witnessing in American society, it is still not permissible for women to have careers and be passionate mothers at the same time.

In her book, a sensitive and intelligent exploration of why women want to take care of their children, Dr. Marneffe gives voice to a deeply felt and rarely addressed conflict that goes to the heart of the emotional struggles of many breadwinning wives. "The second I had my son it changed things," says Inga, whose husband, Kurt, has been out of work for three years. "I was so overwhelmed by the need this child had for me, and even more surprised by my desire to be with him. I want to be a mother—not full-time, mind you, but I want to be home more than I am now." She pauses, then adds vehemently: "Having a baby made me want to stop tiptoeing around the subject of Kurt's unemployment and say to him, 'Get a job. I don't care what it is. Just get a damn job!' "

Inga is the mother of a newborn baby, and most new mothers are passionately obsessed with their infants. It's perfectly normal—and may actually be necessary for the baby's healthy emotional development. The first year of her baby's life is always the most difficult and painful for a working mother. But men have a hard time, too. Just as a woman experiences an immediate emotional and psychological change in herself when she gives birth, so the husband witnesses this change. He is in awe of his wife as she mothers their child. But he may feel like he is on the outside looking in and not know exactly where he fits in his expanded family. He's become a father, an extraordinary and wonderful experience for a man, but he has temporarily lost a wife, helpmate, nurturer, and lover. New parents need to talk about this phenomenon together. New mothers need to explain to their husbands that their preoccupation with the baby is normal and necessary. They also need to let them know that they are counting on their husbands for a feeling of protection, stability, patience, and loving kindness. In other words, a new mother needs her husband to take care of her emotionally while she takes care of their baby.

When women feel unable to fulfill their role as mothers the way they feel they need to, whether that means staying home full-time with their children or simply being there consistently to tuck them in at night, they often experience a sharp flare-up of resentment toward their husbands. Unlike housework, caring for a child is a "chore" that many women want to do and feel compelled to do, at least some of the time.

In our interviews, every single mother said she wished she had more time with her children, but very few said they wanted to be full-time moms. For some, like Leah, the pull toward home is strong and disconcerting, an emotional undertow that is always threatening to sweep them off their feet. For others, it's less intense but ever-present, informing every decision and driving their daily choices—whether to work late, exercise, run errands, or socialize with friends. Once "provider" women have a baby, they may resent their husband's lack of child-care help, because the needs of children add to the already heavy burden of their second, housekeeping shift at home. But they also feel angry about his lack of financial support—often for the first time in their relationship—because their economic responsibility is the force that continually pulls them away from their children. Here again, we have no role models to teach us what to do. Although the mother's feelings are understandable—she does *need* to be with her baby—her anger at her husband is unfair because neither one of them anticipated the profound changes that a baby would bring when they agreed to—or fell into—their financial arrangements.

If you are a couple in this situation, the most important thing to do is to talk about your feelings, frankly and honestly, because it's critical for each of you to have a sense of what the other person is going through. Then, try to show some compassion for each other. Let your spouse know you understand how he feels, and express your sadness and frustration without resorting to blaming or accusations. Acknowledge that this is a difficult time and try to be as loving and patient with each other as you can possibly be.

What is this powerful force we call maternal instinct? Although mothers don't universally respond to giving birth by becoming nurturing toward their infants, the majority do—and not just in the human species. Most female mammals have an innate need to care for their young, to feed and protect them—indeed, the maternal instinct is probably nature's simple, yet elegant, way of ensuring the survival of the species. Science has yet to trace the tangled roots of maternal longing to their source, and theories are as diverse as the authors who espouse them—this one says it's the result of genetic programming; that one points to societal training; yet another one makes the case for a hormonal basis. We believe it's probably a mix of all three. For instance, experts say that in mammals the hormonal brew of pregnancy is in large part responsible for early mother-infant bonding, and oxytocin, a hormone that causes uterine contractions and is released whenever a woman nurses, promotes a feeling of calm as well as pair bonding. In a study of domestic sheep, University of Cambridge researchers found that oxytocin is triggered during a baby's delivery. If the hormone is blocked, the ewe rejects her lamb.

In addition, there's a psychological shift that often occurs when partners become parents. Studies have shown that the transition can cause both women's and men's expectations about gender roles to become more traditional. Many men expect and want their wives to assume the role of primary caregiver for their children, even if the women work full-time. And of course, as we've noted several times, many women have an unanticipated urge to spend more time with their children and, as a result, suddenly wish their lower-earning husbands would step up to the traditional provider plate. This is not to say that breadwinning mothers start to fantasize about finding a new, high-earning mate. Although some might, usually having a child actually bonds couples more closely. But the increased stress of having a child and the extraordinary desire to be with the child often causes a dramatic shift in attitude about their husband's adequacy and reliability as a provider and helpmate.

Because of the ambivalence many women feel toward their situation, talking about the issue can prove tricky. For couples who came of age in the era of feminism not only do their feelings often catch them by surprise, but also, as Marneffe points out, the feelings can be hard to articulate. Even in our child-centered culture, it's considered less than politically correct for women—especially successful professional women—to admit that they feel the emotional pull of motherhood. There is a definite disconnect between widely held beliefs and attitudes toward women and their children.

In *Maternal Desire* Marneffe writes, "Partly owing to five decades of feminist writing, women's sexual desire no longer comes as much of a surprise. Maternal desire, by contrast, has become increasingly problematic. It is almost as if women's desire for sex and their desire to mother have switched places in terms of taboo." Perhaps women have worked so hard for the advances they have achieved politically and financially that it behooves them to keep quiet about the other side of the coin. Women are afraid of giving up what they have already won.

Acknowledging, to yourself and your partner, that your maternal longings exist and are normal is the first step toward coming to a workable solution. Part of that means accepting that you have competing needs within yourself—the need to be a fully autonomous professional woman and the desire to immerse yourself in the role of parent. Next, it's important to admit that because of this internal conflict, you may be sending some confusingly contradictory messages to your partner. Simply pulling that concept from the hidden recesses of your psyche and exposing it to the light of day can be a relief and will give your spouse a better sense of what you're going through.

In the rest of the chapter we'll explain how to air these feelings productively as well as explore a number of ways to fulfill your personal and financial needs for work while also satisfying your thirst to be the kind of parent you long to be. But first, let's examine the impact of children on marriages in general.

WHAT HAPPENS TO YOU TWO WHEN
BABY MAKES THREE?

A "grenade." That's the word Nora Ephron uses in her novel *Heartburn* to describe a baby and its effect on relationships. "When you have a baby, you set off an explosion in your marriage, and when the dust settles, your marriage is different from what it was," she writes.

Ephron was writing from personal experience, but her sentiment resonates with most contemporary couples. Even couples who have adjusted fairly easily to the wife-as-breadwinner scenario may be thrown into turmoil when they have children. Studies have shown, in fact, that the stress and sleeplessness of having a first child actually make this one of the most common times for couples to split up.

John Gottman, Ph.D., codirector and cofounder of the Seattle Marital and Family Institute, and his colleagues followed 130 couples through their first several years of marriage. They found that in the first year after a baby arrives, nearly 70 percent of wives experience a dramatic drop in marital satisfaction. For the husband, the dissatisfaction usually kicks in later, in reaction, Gottman says, to his wife's unhappiness.

In *The Seven Principles for Making Marriage Work*, Gottman explains the problem this way: "There are wide-ranging reasons for this deep disgruntlement—lack of sleep, feeling overwhelmed and unappreciated, the awesome responsibility of caring for such a helpless little creature, juggling motherhood with a job, economic stress and lack of time to oneself, among other things. The big mystery is not why 67 percent of new mothers feel so miserable, but why the other 33 percent just seem to sail through the transition to motherhood unscathed."

Children also cause a dramatic lifestyle shift, limiting the amount of time (and money) couples can devote to fun leisure activities, like going to the movies or dining in nice restaurants—a situation that can reduce the satisfaction quotient in your marriage. (We'll explore this topic in greater detail in the next chapter.)

When women who make more money than their husbands become parents, the stressors are even more acute. "Having kids has made everything more intense for Richard and me," admits Margaret, the personal life coach we introduced at the beginning of chapter 2. "It increased my desire for security, for him to be more of a provider and take care of the kids and me, and it made me expect more help from him in other aspects of our lives—with household chores and daily errands. It also made me wish I had more time to be home with my kids, another thing I never would have expected."

For nontraditional couples, having children introduces numerous logistical problems: Who will supervise homework? Make lunches? Drive car pool? Ferry kids to after-school activities? Who attends the parent/teacher conferences, school plays, and athletic events? Who is on call if a child gets sick or has a doctor's appointment?

In many couples we spoke with, the wife still assumes most of these responsibilities, even though her career is the one that's most important to the family finances—a situation that can cause resentment to flare and prevent men from realizing their full potential as parents.

"A real point of contention for us is that Kevin will say, 'Just tell me what to do,'" says Jane, the corporate-image consultant we wrote about in chapter 2 who recently moved to the suburbs to relieve some of the stress in their lives. "His attitude irks me, because I think he should be able to see what needs to be done as easily as I can. It's not rocket science. If it's five-thirty, you need to prepare dinner."

Kevin's attitude, which was fairly common among the husbands of breadwinning wives we interviewed, conveys the underlying assumption that she is in charge, that the parenting duties are really hers, and that, while he'll help out, he's only filling in for her. Indeed, studies show that working women continue to shoulder most of the burden of child care. Suzanne Bianchi and her colleagues at the University of Maryland found that fathers in 1965 reported spending about one quarter the amount of time engaged in child care as mothers. By 1998, fathers were spending about 55 percent as much time engaged in child care as their wives. Tellingly, the change wasn't because mothers decreased their amount of time with kids; they continued to spend the same amount of time—or even increase their time—despite their husbands' increased participation.

In the next section we'll explore why parenting doesn't come as naturally to some men as to others, but it's important to note here that, apart from lightening your load, there's a very good reason to encourage your husband to become more involved in parenting: Studies show that how your spouse adjusts to parenthood is a key to marital happiness. In fact, Gottman has found that one of the primary criteria separating well-adjusted, happy mothers from struggling ones is their husbands' reaction to being a parent. "It has everything to do with whether the husband experiences the transformation to parenthood along with his wife or gets left behind," he writes.

WHY SOME MEN AREN'T INSTA-DADS

It's a commonly held perception that the nurturing and hands-on care required of parents doesn't come naturally to many men. But do women have a monopoly on the "nurturing instinct"? Although many women we spoke with would say the answer is yes, some experts who have studied fathers in depth offer a different view.

"Once we look closely, we see nurturing skills in both mothers and fathers," says Kyle Pruett, M.D., a clinical professor of psychiatry at Yale Child Study Center and Medical School, in his book *Fatherneed: Why Father Care Is as Essential as Mother Care for Your Child.* "In fact, the very essence of nurturing—the ability to be selfless and patient, loving yet consistent, tolerant but expectant, and, above all, the capacity to share and make sacrifices of one's own emotional, spiritual, material, intellectual assets—ultimately transcends gender."

That said, men today are carrying lots of cultural and emotional baggage that they need to sort through in order to fulfill their role as attentive fathers. Most men, for instance, weren't raised to think of themselves as nurturing, partly because society doesn't sanction the idea of men as caregivers—it's not a common image on television, in the movies, or in magazines, newspapers, or books. Moreover, many were raised by absent or emotionally unavailable fathers, so they lack positive male role models. And even if they had loving, attentive fathers, men still identify the role of parent with providing, with bringing home a paycheck, rather than with hands-on, in-the-trenches caretaking.

Nicholas Townsend, who conducted in-depth interviews with thirty-nine men for his book, *The Package Deal: Marriage, Work and Fatherhood in Men's Lives,* writes: "Fatherhood, as one element of the package deal, is itself composed of four facets: emotional closeness, provision, protection and endowment. Of these four, men said the most important thing they did for their children was to provide for them. This identification of fatherhood and providing is crucial, reflecting the central place of employment in men's sense of self-worth. . . . But there are other things, not directly material, that fathers want: to be emotionally close with their children; to protect their children from threats, fears and dangers; and to endow their children with opportunities and attributes that contribute to their life chances."

The upshot: Men who are no longer playing the provider role have a golden opportunity to hone their skills as parents. But while many men feel a strong urge to be connected, available parents, they also may feel less than confident in their ability to fill the role.

For instance, Will, whom we introduced in chapter 1, would seem to be a natural-born dad. A social worker who has dealt with troubled kids for years, he has an egalitarian attitude toward housework and is supportive of his wife, Tara's, high-paying career as a veterinarian. And yet he says he worries that he doesn't have the patience to stay home with a toddler and is concerned about not bringing in any money—not, he says, because he needs to do so to feel fulfilled as a man, but because he needs to do so to feel content with himself. "I guess I feel more at home in the work world," he admits. Women, actually, should understand this very well, because before the women's movement led to the changes we are all living through now, many women felt a longing for greater personal fulfillment than they found staying home with children.

It is this conflict that contributes to Will's insecurity about his competency as a loving nurturer. He is feeling some resentment and frustration at his situation, so it's important for Tara to be sympathetic to his concerns. Will, in turn, should try to figure out what he might be able to do to feel more fulfilled personally. Tara can also improve the situation by reassuring Will that however restless he might feel, in her eyes he is a wonderful father.

WHEN WOMEN DON'T WANT TO SHARE

When a man's lack of parental confidence (or lack of initiative to learn to become competent) is coupled with his wife's unwillingness to give up parental control, it can prevent him from fully embracing fatherhood. Virginia, thirty-eight, a director of advertising sales for a television station, admits that she jealously guards her time with their toddler. "I love taking care of Sam and never want to give up a minute of it," she says. "Nothing is as important as that right now. My house isn't the cleanest place, but I figure I have a choice: I can clean the stove or sit on the floor and play with Sam. In my mind, there's no contest."

While her devotion is heartwarming—and understandable, given the fact that she's away from her son most days of the week—the unexpected consequence is that her husband, Jake, thirty-six, a video editor, feels somewhat left out. "Having a kid definitely changes things. I never thought Virginia would want to be a stay-at-home mom, but I can see now that it would really appeal to her. It's not going to happen, though, because she makes a lot more than I do. I work all day and pitch in around the house after work, but then I sit on the sofa while she takes care of the kid. I don't do much of the child care, because she wants to do it all. I'll sometimes suggest that she go do something on the weekend just so I can spend some time with him."

Sociologist Pepper Schwartz, author of *Love Between Equals: How Peer Marriage Really Works,* was quoted in a *New York Times* story on the topic, saying, "Women may give lip service to wanting husbands who take on an equal role in raising children, but many will pull rank when an important decision, like how to discipline or what babysitter to hire, has to be made."

Why do hardworking wives, who could undoubtedly use the help, brush off their husbands' efforts in the parenting realm? We believe there are two main reasons. For one thing, women see themselves as "natural" caretakers and often feel guilty if they're not filling that role. They have the ghosts of their mothers, grand-mothers, and every other female sitting on their shoulders telling them that they must "do right" by their children. Second, there is the biological urge, closely connected to the societal and maternal reinforcement, that leads women to believe that it is they, and only they, who can totally protect their children from danger. Down deep, mothers believe that no one else can do it as well. But women owe it to themselves, their children, and their partners to accept the fact that men can protect their children from danger, too. Indeed, studies have shown that while men may take a different approach to child rearing—giving kids more independence, for instance—children aren't hurt or injured more frequently on Dad's watch than on Mom's. Even so, many of the women we spoke with said their hus-bands are good about roughhousing and joking around with the children, but when it comes to actually caring for them they often fall short.

"Richard plays with the kids and even bathes them, and reads to them," says Margaret, "but he would be utterly baffled if he had to handle all the day-to-day details—getting the twelve pairs of socks together for camp, remembering to pack the children's lunches, making all the doctor appointments and play dates. I don't think we'll ever be able to share those responsibilities, even though they're incredibly tedious and wear me out.

"There's something about attunement," adds Margaret. "Men are better about dealing with kids than their fathers were, but they have to be willing to give it their full attention, to be really present for all the demands and needs. Richard can walk in the door, get on the computer and check e-mail. I walk in the door and begin taking care of everyone."

Margaret's point is one that many alpha-earner wives echo: Women seem to have a more highly developed ability to multitask and to store infinite amounts of child-related minutiae in their brains than men. Maybe it's because of biology, or perhaps it's simply upbringing—we saw our mothers buzzing around like hummingbirds all day and eventually began to emulate them. Either way, it's a reality in many marriages, and one that becomes more fraught the more a woman earns.

"I don't know whether it's nature or nurture, but guys just aren't on top of things the way women are," says Jane. "I'm extremely organized. It's a skill set I have that Kevin doesn't. I've never seen a man who would be my equal in terms of organizing the haircuts, the allergy appointments, the I-can-only-find-one-fleece-mitten crisis."

Some women grow resentful that they are always the ones who have to register the kids for classes, schedule the checkups and play dates, coordinate babysitting, and handle every other detail of their children's lives. And most men are perfectly comfortable knowing that their wives are in charge of just about everything. They generally feel that mothers "do it better," and are even afraid of screwing up should they actually take charge. The solution? Enlist your husband's help. Make lists for him, or explain exactly what needs to be done, and he will surely pitch in. But don't expect him to notice and act on the fact that your child needs a haircut or a new winter coat. If he's never done it before, he's not going to change overnight. Express your gratitude for the things he does bring to the table, and he's more likely to keep doing them—and maybe more.

Research shows that dads and babies benefit when they spend time alone, away from Mom's watchful eyes. A study conducted by researchers at the National Institute of Mental Health found that a father and his infant develop an enhanced relationship through interactions that occur between the two of them in the absence of the mother. They also found that such time alone builds and enhances a father's skills. Experts like Dr. Pruett say the male influence is important for raising healthy children. Research by him and other child-development experts has shown that fathers tend to be less predictable and more playful in their approach to children. They encourage their children to explore the world around them, and they tend to use more complex speech with children, even young ones, than mothers do. What many women fail to recognize is that men have a different skill set—one that they may not display if women take full responsibility for all the child care.

Anne, the small-business owner, says, "One night a few months ago, Barry took our four-year-old to a basketball game. He didn't give him dinner beforehand and then bought him popcorn and cotton candy at the game. When they came home, my son announced that Daddy had cleaned his little face with beer. My son loved it! I would have had wipes, healthy snacks, and a sippy cup of milk for him. But it was totally fine by me that one night that month, he didn't eat a perfectly balanced, healthy meal." Anne recognizes the importance not only of the father-child bonding time but also of exposing her children to a parenting influence other than her own. But this hasn't always been the case. "For a long time, I was annoyed that I was in charge of the caretaking—the meals, the baths, the bedtimes—and Barry could pop in for an hour, wrestle around on the floor, and be a hero. I wasn't getting how important it was for the kids, and Barry, to have that unfettered playtime. And as soon as I started acknowledging to Barry how much I appreciated his parenting, he began voluntarily pitching in on the caretaking stuff. I also had to admit to myself that I enjoyed the caretaking—that there's something incredibly special and intimate about bathing the kids and putting them to bed. I don't want to wrestle, but they need that just as much as they need to be fed a healthy meal."

Most women say their husbands are great at horsing around with the kids, but they acknowledge this in a dismissive manner. The wrestling, chasing, tickling, and physical play that comes so naturally to fathers is critical for children, too, and is a legitimate and valuable parenting contribution.

Not only do men learn to be better parents when they're given the opportunity to be alone with their children, but kids benefit as well. Says Dr. Pruett in *Fatherneed,* "Infants who have time alone with Dad show richer social and exploratory behavior than children not exposed to such experiences. They smile more frequently in general, and they more frequently present toys to their dad. They also spend more time looking at and manipulating objects as part of heightened exploratory behavior." A dad's involvement also may enhance children's verbal skills, help them feel more competent at school, foster the development of empathy, and encourage them to embrace more liberal attitudes toward gender roles.

Just as being a good mother doesn't necessarily mean spending all day every day with your little one, being an involved father doesn't require a full-time commitment. But it does require focus and attention, and a real desire to be emotionally present and engaged when spending time in kids' company.

Says Dr. Pruett, "Over and over again in the science of father care, researchers point out that it is the *quality* of interaction between father and child—that is, whether the father is sensitive to the child's needs and reactions—that determines the overall value of his involvement in his child's life, not the *quantity*. Counting the minutes that child and father are in each other's company tells us very little about the ultimate influence of the father on the development of his child."

How a man shows his love for his children is ultimately the most important factor in his parenting. But a father also needs to be physically present in children's lives. Father and children need to be friends, they need to know each other, and they need to develop close emotional and psychological bonds. Working fathers should try to spend time alone with their children on weekends, even if it's only a couple of hours. It's sometimes hard for working mothers to allow for this because of their own ambivalence. Remind yourself that you need time to be alone—something most working moms sacrifice all too readily—and that your husband and child need time together. By building father-child time into your weekend schedule you'll not only promote their bonding but also sow the seeds of a stronger parenting partnership.

GETTING PAST GUILT (AND GUILTMONGERS)

"I never envisioned myself being the provider once we had kids," admits Virginia, "but there are some days I think it's great, when I love the feeling of having so much responsibility for our family. But when I drop Sam off at day care, it's hard for me not to feel torn. At those moments I inevitably think, 'I'm a terrible mother,' and I wish I could just stay home and be with him."

Like figuring out how to discreetly operate a breast pump and learning how to give a professional presentation on three hours of sleep, guilt seems to be an unavoidable part of the working-mother package. Women are hardwired to be first responders when they have a child, and it's virtually impossible for them to turn off that instinct the moment they pick up their briefcase and head out the door—nor would most women realistically want to. But they would like to be able to do so without the added burden of guilt, the emotional scourge of high-achieving women. Guilt comes not just from within, from the natural concern about doing what's best for the child, but also from society, from the audible *tsk-tsk*ing of other parents, friends, relatives, and neighbors who hold more traditional views on motherhood.

As Nicholas Townsend writes in *The Package Deal:* "Mothers in the United States are expected to be active participants in their children's daily lives, to satisfy their needs and wants, to love unconditionally, and to 'be there,' physically and emotionally for their children. When they do all these things they are seen as acting appropriately."

Later he adds, "Using the words 'parent' and 'parenting' to conceal gendered activity and gendered blame is also a feature of public discourse. When we hear, for instance, that children are unsupervised because 'parents' are not at home when they come home from school, or that 'parents' are putting careers before children, the reference is clearly to mothers, since fathers are *supposed* to be working away from the home."

In their recent book, *The Mommy Myth: The Idealization of Motherhood and How It Has Undermined Women,* authors Susan Douglas and Meredith Michaels make the case that media messages about "good" mothers have reached a fevered pitch in the past twenty-five years—and mothers' guilt levels have followed suit. They say that, thanks to the media, "mothers are subjected to an onslaught of beatific imagery, romantic fantasies, self-righteous sermons, psychological warnings, terrifying movies about losing their children, even more terrifying news stories about abducted and abused children, and totally unrealistic advice about how to be the most perfect and revered mom in the neighborhood, maybe even the whole country."

The authors believe that, while most of us recognize that the scripted and airbrushed moms portrayed in the media are unattainable ideals, those images still linger in the back of our minds, causing us to question our choices, berate ourselves for our failings, and feel eternally lacking in our ability to raise healthy children.

"We know that building a scale model of Versailles out of mashed potatoes may not be quite as crucial to good mothering as *Martha Stewart Living* suggests," Douglas and Michaels write. "Yet here we are, cowed by that most tyrannical of our cultural icons, *Perfect Mom.*" They also suggest that the media's messages have created two opposing camps—stay-at-home mothers and working ones—and pitted them against each other in a lose-lose battle in which full-time mothers are condemned for being boring and unfulfilled while working moms are castigated for being cold, neglectful, and unfeminine.

The women we spoke with all have tales from the front of the so-called mommy wars. Virginia says that many of her closest women friends are stay-at-home moms, so she's often on the receiving end of e-mails about 11 A.M. park play dates she couldn't possibly make and mommy-and-me classes she'll never get to attend. But what hurts more deeply are the verbal barbs, intentional or not. "The other day, a couple of the women in one of the play groups I'm in on the weekend were talking about putting their kids to bed at six-thirty, and I said I put Sam down at eight. They looked at me like I was a monster and said, 'How could you? Sleep is so important for kids this age.' Then, they said, 'Oh, that's right. You work. You wouldn't get to see him at all if you didn't let him stay up later, huh?' I don't know if they intended to be mean, but their comments really stung."

There are several ways to blunt the impact of wrenching guilt. One is to recognize that it's a normal emotion—and that it's probably not a sign that you're doing something wrong. Women feel guilty for all sorts of things they shouldn't—doing things for themselves, speaking their minds, saying no to unreasonable demands. The guilt of working mothers is simply a symptom of conflicting emotions. Even stay-at-home moms suffer from guilt. They worry that they haven't paid enough attention to their children or aren't feeding them the most healthful food. They also fret over not challenging themselves professionally. In other words, guilt isn't the curse of working women, it's the curse of women in general. When friends who are stay-at-home mothers say hurtful things, it can be helpful to recognize that they may be envious or defensive about their choice to stay home—and to see themselves as less interesting and modern. They may want to make you feel like a bad parent because you have something that they don't have: independence, success, and a separate life—one they imagine to be more glamorous and exciting than their own.

Know that different people make different choices. Understand that your marriage is on the leading edge of a trend—and many people's attitudes have yet to catch up. That doesn't mean your approach is wrong. It simply means that it's less common, and because of that, you're bound to get some flak.

Some women have learned to deal with the guilt and judgment by looking for personal validation in other ways. Kimberly, Steve's wife, says, "The stay-at-home moms still look down on me. They can't believe I'd let my husband stay home rather than stay home myself. At first their attitude really surprised me. You'd think people would be more open-minded about alternative families. But I feel happy with our arrangement, for the most part. I have a strong sense of self. I may not get the approval of full-time moms, but I get so much approval at work that it balances out."

If you're feeling shaky about your own sense of self and what you really want, it can be helpful to take a fearless internal inventory of your strengths and weaknesses so you can determine realistically whether you'd be more suited to staying home. Many of the women we spoke with acknowledged that, although they felt deeply torn about being away from their children, they wouldn't survive life as stay-at-home moms.

"If I were a full-time mom, I would eat my young," says Christina, forty-four, a casting director. "I stayed home for six months with my first child, and it was a wake-up call to me. It was nice to have the opportunity, because it helped me exorcize the guilt demon a little bit. I don't have to say 'What if.' I know the answer. I have the tremendous emotional liberation of knowing that I'm a better mom if I work."

Even so, Christina, who lives in an affluent suburb of Boston where many mothers don't work outside the home, acknowledges that the daily disapproval of her friends and neighbors gets under her skin. "I actually put my son in private school in the city partly because I couldn't deal with the moms in the suburbs," she says. "I might as well be a third gender as far as they're concerned. When my daughter was in preschool, I got calls saying, 'Can you be here at ten A.M. for tea?' even though they knew I worked. I wanted to say, 'Are you calling all the dads and asking them this question?' "

By the time her daughter entered elementary school, Christina had had enough of the incessant badgering. The last straw came when she asked the principal at her daughter's school about after-school programs and the principal replied, without a shred of remorse, "Moms in our town don't work." Sending her child to school out of the area has given her a certain amount of emotional freedom, she says. "I realized that if we stayed in the local public school, I was always going to be the bad mom," she says. "I couldn't stand the idea of having all those women frowning at me in the grocery store. Sartre said hell is other people. For working moms, hell is other parents."

For most breadwinning mothers the most gut-wrenching issue is the concern that anything other than mother care is bad for kids, so the surest way out of the morass of guilt is to address the issue of child care head-on. Overwhelmingly, studies reveal that the most important factor in children's well-being is their overall relationship with their parents, both their father and mother, regardless of whether they work or not. As Lynne Casper and Suzanne Bianchi point out in *Continuity and Change in the American Family*, "Given the effort that has been devoted to searching for negative effects of maternal employment on children's academic achievement and emotional adjustment, the paucity of findings (either positive or negative) is surprising."

Finding good child care that you trust and can rely on can help relieve the burden of guilt for many high-earning moms. "I have a great nanny, and I've really come to believe that children benefit from having different caretakers," says Margaret, the life coach. "Taking care of children is hard and lonely work. One of the burdens we carry is this mythology of being the perfect stay-at-home mom, yet if many of us did it, we'd be miserable."

Anne, the small-business owner, makes another valid point: "Every minute with my kids is precious and rich, and when I'm home, I am completely focused on them. I don't really believe I could pack that much quality time into a full day. I'm sure I would be pretty unpleasant for a lot of the time, actually, if I was home all day."

It's important for parents to keep in mind that in the past, women were rarely at home alone with children. They had the support and help of an extended family and neighbors. Historically, child care was a communal effort. It's only in relatively recent years that families in the United States have become so spread out, that children and grandchildren live far away from their parents, grandparents, aunts, uncles, and cousins. Today's family is a nuclear family, alone and terribly overburdened. That's nobody's fault, and certainly not yours.

When Margaret starts feeling guilty about her overburdened situation and resentful of her husband for not making more money to ease her load, she tries to remind herself of the advantages she has. "I'm really very lucky to have a husband who supports me in all my roles, not just the traditional ones. When I remember that, I feel grateful instead of guilty. He gives me the opportunity to be in the world in a way other than as a mother. If you can find those points of gratitude, it can help."

It's important to try to keep a positive outlook, to see that the glass is half full. Remember that in your work and career you have an opportunity to use your intellect and fulfill yourself in ways that would not be possible without the help of your husband, and that your life can indeed be far richer and more interesting than it might have been had you chosen to stay home. In addition, you are serving as an important role model for your own children.

ONE SOLUTION TO THE CHILD-CARE DILEMMA: THE STAY-AT-HOME DAD

What happens when a man steps into the traditional woman's shoes and the role reversal comes full circle? We found that the couples who are happiest with the situation are the ones who discussed it ahead of time and chose it for themselves. But, as Sasha and Kiernan found, there's really no way to know for sure how you're going to feel until you're there.

Sasha, thirty-eight, a real estate attorney, and Kiernan, thirty-nine, a software salesman, were married for five years before she started making more money than he, and it's always been "a non-issue," according to Sasha. "It helps that a lot of our friends are in the same position," she says.

Even so, when they got pregnant two years ago and Kiernan offered to quit his job to stay home, Sasha was taken aback. "I had a visceral negative reaction," she recalls. "I said, 'If anyone's going to stay home, it's going to be me.' I felt like I'd rather hire a nanny than have him stay home. The thought of it made me feel very jealous and territorial. I think I felt the baby had to love me more because I'm the mom."

After their son was born, she took a four-month maternity leave, during which Kiernan lost his job. "He stayed home for six months after I did, and we both had a total attitude reversal," she says. "He realized that staying home with a child isn't something that would make him feel fulfilled, and I realized that I was okay with it." Kiernan has since found a job, and Sasha has found a nanny she "adores," so they're both happy with the situation. "After staying home for four months, I know my strengths and weaknesses," she says. "I love my child, but I'm better at working than I am at being a full-time mom."

Even among happy SAHDs the situation "takes a little getting used to," admits Steve, the stay-at-home dad we profiled in chapter 2. "I went from sitting in a boardroom with a bunch of finance geeks to singing baby songs. I was okay with Kimberly being out in the work world—that was the choice we both agreed to—but it was a bit difficult on a personal level at first."

Most of Steve's friends predicted that he'd be back to work in a few weeks, that his experiment with full-time fatherhood would flame out faster than you could say "diaper change," but he's lasted seven years. "I had headhunters calling and saying, 'You can't believe the amount of money I could get you if you'd come back,'" he recalls. "It was hard to pass up, but not as hard as you might expect. I've really grown into this role. In the beginning, it all seemed a little foreign, but I feel as competent as any mom now, even if I don't do things exactly like the women I know."

Other SAHDs express similar notions. They see themselves not so much as fathers trying to be mothers, but rather as fathers being full-time parents—men carving out a whole new niche for themselves at home, complete with its own learning curve, advantages and drawbacks, and unique approaches.

Clay, the poker player we introduced in chapter 1, says he feels very competent as a parent but he sometimes gets the impression that the mothers he encounters question his ability. "It's usually from women I don't even know," he says. "For example, I always have the children dressed in fewer layers than their friends, and some moms will make comments about how they're not dressed warmly enough. I try not to let it bother me too much. My kids are healthy and happy, so I must be doing something right."

Clay is lucky because he has a good relationship with his wife, Sarah, and he can talk to her about his run-ins with stay-at-home moms and she can reassure him. Sarah doesn't object to the way he parents, even though his approach is somewhat different from hers. "He's great with the kids, but there are differences between a mother and a father. I'm a little more affectionate, while he's more playful. He goofs around with them more. But if one of them falls down or gets hurt, I'm the one they run to for comforting."

She accepts the fact that they approach the job differently, and tries not to step in and take charge when she sees him doing something she doesn't like. "I try to remind myself that this is his job and I can't always be second-guessing his choices," she says. It also helps, she says, to remind herself of the sacrifices he's made by staying home. "I'm way into my job, and I knew I'd never leave it to stay home with the kids," she says. "I feel fortunate to have a husband who was willing to give up his career, and I try not to lose sight of that."

The idea of giving up control of parenting can be difficult for many women, however. For the many reasons that we've enumerated, handing over responsibility for child care to anyone, even to the father of her child, is scary and threatening to a mother, not only in terms of her identity as a woman but in terms of the safety of her children.

Some women who were raised with traditional values may find that being the family provider is a role that feels just plain wrong. Stacy, an advertising executive, and Mike, whom we introduced in chapter 1, don't have children yet. But after his stint of unemployment, Mike told Stacy he'd be willing to be a stay-at-home dad. "For me that's scary," says Stacy. "I've never thought I'd be the primary breadwinner once I have kids. I'm happy to do it now, when it's just the two of us, but I can't imagine being the one who leaves for work in the morning when we have children. Maybe it's because I grew up in a very traditional family. My dad was a stockbroker, and my mom stayed at home with me and my four siblings. I love my career, but I've always thought of it as for me and for now. I don't know how I'd feel about it if I had no way out, if I had a family counting on me. That's a ton of pressure."

Even women who've adjusted well to their provider status say there are kinks in the system. Sarah struggles with the fact that there's no downtime between her day job and parenting duties. "I'm sometimes really tired when I get home from work, but Clay is tired from watching the kids, so I have to take over," she says. "I don't get any downtime. It's not his fault. It's just the way it is."

Jill, whose husband, Johnny, is a SAHD, is in the same boat, a problem that bugs her more because her husband finds time for leisure despite his parental responsibilities. "He has the kids at his parents' house probably once a week. That makes me jealous, because he has more free time than I do. But he's better about asking for help than I am. Women are trained to do everything themselves. Men know how to delegate."

Indeed, delegating at home is a skill most women, but especially high-achieving career women, have a hard time mastering. One reason may be overcompensation for not being the primary caretaker; another reason is that many successful women learned early on that they needed to take care of themselves without asking for help. Whatever the reason, women must learn to delegate at home if they want to find peace of mind in their busy lives.

CARVING OUT SOME TIME FOR YOURSELF

"I never do anything alone," says Leah. "I never go shopping. My wardrobe looks like hell. I was an exercise fanatic until I had two kids, but now I'm a flabby, out-of-shape mess. That's one of the biggest tolls of our situation. Because I work so much I'm not willing to sacrifice my time with my kids for anything else—to do things alone or to spend time with Frank. It's probably unhealthy, but there are only so many hours in a day, and I have to prioritize."

The time crunch is a recurring theme for mothers who make more money than their husbands. Most of the women we spoke with said they'd pared their personal time down to the bare minimum. "I'm lucky if I shower every other day," says Claire. Yet, having time to yourself is essential for recharging your batteries, because the potential for burnout is high. Not only are breadwinning wives responsible for the family's financial well-being, but they also tend to do more of the housework and serve as CEO of the child care. It's probably not an exaggeration to say that women who are primary breadwinners are carrying more day-to-day responsibilities than any group of people, male or female, in history—except, perhaps, single parents.

The price of such a lifestyle can be steep: Studies have shown that long-term stress can cause everything from headaches and fatigue to low sex drive and decreased tolerance for frustration, as well as serious illness. The trouble is, for most high-achieving women, self-care is the last thing on their to-do list. They're so busy meeting obligations and everyone else's needs, they often let their own health and well-being slide.

In her book *Self-Nurture: Learning to Care for Yourself as Effectively as You Care for Everyone Else,* Alice Domar, Ph.D., writes, "The simple but devastating message that we're brought up to believe is that if we nurture ourselves we're being selfish." That is, other people come first. But women who take the time to give some loving attention to themselves are not only happier and less stressed but also are better parents and partners. With those benefits in mind, it only makes sense to try to get in the habit of nurturing yourself.

If you're struggling with the idea, start small: Take five-minute breaks in the day, during which you do nothing more strenuous than breathe; commit to a twenty-minute walk at lunchtime; ask the nanny to stay an extra half hour several days a week so you can do something relaxing: get a manicure or massage, read a novel, knit, call a friend and talk, or take a bath. Enlist your husband's help as well, by explaining how tired you feel and asking him to commit to taking the kids for a couple of hours every weekend. Remind him (and yourself!) how important it is for the children to spend playtime alone with him. And be sure to tell him that knowing your kids are with him helps alleviate some of your guilt over taking time for yourself.

Of all the stress-reduction tools available, exercise is probably the best. It can help relieve anxiety and depression, it makes you physically healthier, it can boost your sex drive, and it can enhance everything from your daily energy to your self-esteem. And, as Anne, who used to run marathons, has found, if all else fails, you can do it with your children. "I've taken to walking around the city with my kids," she says. "It's not exactly a substitute for regular running, but it makes me feel good—and it's good for them, too."

Another key to carving out time for yourself is simply learning to say no. Know your limits. Know that you don't have to be and do everything for everyone. And believe (because it's true) that if you make time for a massage or bike ride, or whatever makes you happy, you'll be in better shape to nurture your kids and even your spouse, and everyone will be happier.

FAMILY-STRENGTHENING SOLUTIONS

When women who make more money than their husbands have children, couples often find creative ways to adapt their lifestyles to meet everyone's needs. Bob and Carla, whom we introduced in chapter 2, take the tag-team approach to parental duty. They both work, but since he works at night, he is home with their two children during the day. "It's a win-win situation," he says. "We have two incomes, and we have a parent home with the kids. The downside is we're often tired and we don't get to spend any time alone as a couple." Carla agrees that the situation works well, and she accepts that some drawbacks are unavoidable. "He leaves within five to ten minutes of when I get home, so sometimes I feel like a single parent," she says. "But right now I wouldn't have it any other way. I feel good about the fact that we're both equally involved in our children's lives."

Even women with less-than-helpful husbands have found ways to make their lives run more smoothly. Anne's biggest complaint was that when she got home she wasn't able to enjoy her children's company because she was thrown into the role of family cook, house straightener, child bather, and "general all-around drill sergeant." Her solution: "I started having my nanny bathe and feed the kids dinner before I get home so I can spend quality time with them before bed," she says. "Now, instead of rushing around and feeling stressed, I get to play games and talk with them. I'm much more relaxed, and I'm sure they are, too."

Because Rose, whom we mentioned in chapter 3, was forever angry at her husband, Mason, for flaking out on his commitments to the family, they set up a system to avoid such mishaps. "We each have our own calendars," she says, "plus we keep a family calendar in the kitchen for stuff like doctors' appointments, so everyone knows what the fixed obligations are. Then, we set aside some time Sunday night to review the calendars for the upcoming week so we can anticipate potential glitches." Rose has also learned that she needs to ask for help rather than expect Mason to see what she needs. She now says things like "I'm feeling very squeezed about the birthday party coming up. Will you buy the invitations and get them sent by next Sunday for me?"

Couples who have set aside time for family rituals and try to inject a sense of spirituality into their lives also seem happier with their situation. Parents who go to church or synagogue with the family and incorporate some of the rituals into their home life have an easier time coping with marital stress—including stress brought on by unequal earning status. It gives both partners a broader perspective on life, as well as a sense of sharing and togetherness. And the associated rituals—church on Sunday, shabbos dinner on Friday—are times for the whole family to be together that everyone can count on.

But some of the problems facing breadwinning mothers may simply be inherent in the job, as much a part of the grind as time constraints and stress. The happiest breadwinning wives we spoke with accept their lives and try to do the best they can with their situation. "We're a perfect role reversal," says Cheryl, forty-four, a vice president at a large accounting firm. "Carl retired in 1995, when our kids were one and three, to be a stay-at-home dad, and it's worked out great. He's got the right temperament for the job. He coaches the kids' basketball teams, grocery shops, does the laundry and the housework. But we also have a nanny come in several days a week to help out so he can play golf and do the things he wants to do. I don't want him to be stuck in the role of the 1950s housewife. They weren't happy, so why would I expect him to be?"

Cheryl says their arrangement works because she and Carl are 180 degrees opposite. "He's a quiet strength," she says. "I'm direct and high-powered. He listens first, then moves forward. I'm all action." Does she worry that he's spending more time with their children, or that she isn't spending enough? "I'm relieved that he's home, because it lets me concentrate on my career with less guilt," she says. "If I'm being totally honest, I have to admit that I'm a little tortured about not being there for my kids. I'm not as involved as I'd like to be, and I feel a little cheated about that. But life is all about sacrifices and trade-offs, right? I could have made a lot more money than I have, but I took a less aggressive piece of the business because I wanted to have more balance. You can't have it all, and once you accept that, life seems a little less stressful. We've tried to make the choices that felt right to us, and I think we've done a pretty good job."

FIVE

Couple Time:
Romance And Sex

Sex?" says Sharon, thirty-nine, a note of incredulity in her voice. "What's that??" Then she laughs, but she admits she's only half joking. "When you have huge financial and professional obligations as well as kids at home, romance isn't exactly a priority." While she understands intellectually the challenges of their situation, Sharon, who owns a public-relations firm, says she's still sometimes shocked by how much effort it takes to maintain a romantic connection with her husband, Scott, especially considering their steamy early relationship.

They met when they were both living in Southern California. She was twenty-six years old and a poorly paid copywriter at an advertising agency. He was thirty-nine and well established in his career as a creative director. "We had a whirlwind romance—lots of romantic dinners and exciting weekends away," she says. "I loved that he was older and successful, already established in his career. I thought he was going to take care of me for the rest of my life. He's such a loving, nurturing man."

So swept away was she that they were engaged after just four months. Shortly thereafter, she got a job offer in New York, and he quit his job to go with her. After staying for a year, however, they both missed Los Angeles, so they moved back across the country and he enrolled in film school—his lifelong dream—while she worked. "At the time, I never thought of myself as the breadwinner," she says. "I thought he was going to school so he could have another career. It was more like I was biding my time until he took over again."

Two years and $100,000 in tuition later, however, their marriage was showing signs of strain. "We were both so busy we were only spending two hours a week together," she says. "We knew we wanted kids, and we decided that if we were going to have them, he should quit school and we should try to get pregnant. It was a little strange, because he became a stay-at-home dad before we actually had children, but that was just the way it worked out."

Now, seven years later, they have two children and a lovely home and Sharon's career is thriving. But their sex life isn't. "I still find Scott very attractive, but there are so many hurdles we have to overcome to get in the mood."

First, she says, there's the incessant pressure of being a breadwinning mom. "It's a thin tightrope you walk when you have so much responsibility, and there's no net," she says. "I can't even talk with some of my closest friends about the pressure I feel because there's no way anyone can understand how it feels unless they're in this position. When my friends who don't have kids say they're busy or tired or stressed out, I feel like saying, 'Ha! What I wouldn't give for your version of stress.'"

It's all too easy, Sharon admits, to let the pressure she feels spill over into resentment toward Scott. "I sometimes feel like saying, 'I'm pulling the wagon for the whole family, and you're sitting in it. I need you to get out and push!' "

But even more troubling, she says, is the strangely asexual sensation created when you swap roles and strip away all the traditional trappings of gender. "It's hard for me to feel feminine when I have to put on armor and go out into the work world every day, and it's hard for Scott to feel masculine when he has to ask me for money and attend mommy-and-me classes," she says. "We've made choices that suit our individual personalities and suit our family but that make our relationship as a man and woman more challenging."

It's often said that a good sex life is the best marriage counselor around, and this is mostly true. Sexual intimacy seems to bond couples, even those who have serious clashes outside the bedroom. On the other hand, if one partner isn't interested in sex, it can create painful feelings of rejection and resentment that often reverberate in every aspect of the relationship.

Like so many of us, Sharon walked into her marriage with unarticulated expectations of what Scott's role would be, whether she knew it or not. Scott was supposed to be the provider, taking care of her materially even when she no longer needed it. She has managed to overcome her outdated expectations about gender roles in many ways, but the proof that those old ideas linger is evident in her conflicted attitude toward sex.

Most of us were raised to believe that our gender roles—the roles we play for the outside world—have something to do with how masculine or feminine we are. They don't—or at least they don't have to unless we let them. Sharon claims to feel asexual, but in reality she's still completely feminine inside. Her femininity is just buried underneath layers of stress, resentment, and probably a little guilt for not behaving like a "good girl." More than anything, she—and all the other breadwinning wives like her—needs her husband to validate her sexuality—to make her feel womanly and desirable, even if at the end of the day there's little time or energy left for sex.

Of course, the flip side is also true. A woman has to let her husband know that she finds him sexually desirable. You can do this with humor, flirting, a kiss, a squeeze, or whatever private sexual "language" the two of you have created.

Sharon and Scott have been in therapy and have worked hard to keep their sexual relationship alive in the face of these obstacles, but she says it's a constant struggle. "Since we're living out these nontraditional roles, we have to try to find ways to make each other feel masculine and feminine," she says. "For instance, last night he made a wonderful dinner. I praised and complimented his effort the same way another wife might acknowledge her husband who's just come home from a successful business presentation. But I had to learn to do that. That's part of the challenge when you're in this situation where you're making more money than your husband. There are no role models. There's no one telling you what to do. You have to come up with your own winning formula in your own marriage, day by day."

But one can hear the disappointment in Sharon's voice because Scott is not coming home after a successful business presentation. Those unmet expectations are also partly responsible for putting her sexual desire into neutral.

A quick perusal of magazine racks and bookstore shelves is enough to tell you that Sharon and Scott aren't alone. *Redbook* magazine asks if we're "Too Stressed for Romance?" A *Newsweek* cover declares "No Sex, Please, We're Married." And books with titles like *The Sex-Starved Marriage: A Couple's Guide to Boosting Their Marriage Libido* and *Rekindling Desire: A Step-by-Step Program to Help Low-Sex and No-Sex Marriages* are selling hundreds of thousands of copies and creating fodder for an endless stream of daytime talk shows, during which couples confess (and lament) their flagging desire.

What's behind this epidemic of low libido? How can couples find ways to reconnect, when there are so many competing demands for their time and energy? Is there a way to leave stress behind at the bedroom threshold? And most important, when you toss traditional gender roles aside, how do you keep the masculine/feminine fires alive?

THE SEXUAL DEFICIT

On average, married couples have sex slightly more than once a week, according to research conducted by the University of Chicago's National Opinion Research Center. But researchers admit that number may not be reliable, because they suspect that even in anonymous polls many people are somewhat less than truthful when the topic is frequency. Who wants to own up to a sexual slump, after all—especially in our highly eroticized world, where everyone, it appears, from our favorite TV characters to the mythical Joneses seems to be doing it on a regular basis?

Thanks to a combination of forces, including the women's movement, the introduction of the birth-control pill, and the onslaught of sexuality research from respected groups like the Kinsey Institute and Masters and Johnson, our attitudes toward sex have undergone a radical transformation in the past thirty years, from "nice girls don't" to "nice girls do . . . and do . . . and do." Sexual desire (and expression) is not only an American birthright, it's a cultural expectation.

As the *Newsweek* cover story notes, "Boomers were the front line of the sexual revolution. They practically invented guilt-free, pre-marital sex, and they know what they're missing better than any previous generation in history." Movies, television shows, and the explosion in the pornography industry can make any of us feel like we are missing out. What we don't seem to realize well enough is that the groans and screams and cries of delight are all acting. Our new openness may be creating an ironic and unexpected backlash of sexual anxiety: We tend to think everyone is having better—and more frequent—sex than we are.

As you read this chapter it's important to keep in mind that there's no accepted medical definition of "normal" sexual activity. A healthy sex life has more to do with satisfaction than statistics. If you and your partner have sex twice a month but you're both happy with your love life and have a vibrant romantic connection, there's no reason to see yourselves as substandard.

That said, there's a widening consensus among experts that many couples are struggling with low libido—and the problem may be growing. Some psychologists estimate that 15 to 20 percent of couples have sex no more than ten times a year, a rate that gives them the dubious distinction of falling into a newly recognized category: the sexless marriage. In the *Newsweek* cover story on the topic, therapist Michele Weiner Davis, author of *The Sex-Starved Marriage*, is quoted as saying that the number of sexless marriages is a "grossly underreported statistic."

We found evidence of the problem in our interviews as well. Many of the women and men we spoke with acknowledged that their sex lives are lacking. They'd like to be doing it more, they said. But they just can't seem to get in the mood—a problem that affects men as well as women but appears to be more common in the latter. According to a study published in the *Journal of the American Medical Association*, 31 percent of men and 43 percent of women suffer sexual problems, including low desire, performance anxiety, premature ejaculation, and/or pain during intercourse.

Meanwhile, drug companies are rushing to find medicinal "cures" for women's woes, a sure sign that there's a hefty market for such products. Although Viagra hasn't proven to be the boon for women that it is for some men, other products will undoubtedly try to fill the gap. The *Newsweek* article reports that Avlimil, an herbal medication designed to help put the drive back in women's sex lives, had sales of 200,000 packages in January 2003, its first month on the market. And six months later the company said it was receiving as many as three thousand calls a day from women who are interested in seeing if the remedy can help them.

What's causing this sexual listlessness? In some people, medical factors may be playing a role. Depression, which affects about nineteen million Americans a year and twice as many women as men, can cause a loss of interest in sex, as can many antidepressants, the most widely prescribed treatment for depression. Hormonal imbalances, including problems with levels of thyroid hormone or testosterone, the main hormone fueling the sex drive in both men and women, may be a factor as well.

But more and more researchers are blaming the plague of low libido on the stress created by having both partners in the workplace—a theory that even spawned its own acronym: DINS, for dual-income, no sex. Juggling numerous roles can overtax both your time and energy, leaving you with little of either at the end of the day. Moreover, the stresses, time constraints, and petty resentments endured by most dual-income couples are often magnified when women step into (and men step away from) the role of material provider. When women shoulder most of the family financial burden *and* have children *and* are the default housekeepers and child-care providers—in effect saying yes to every responsibility that comes down the pike—they may feel that the one thing they *can* say no to is sex.

However, it's interesting to note that one study from the University of Wisconsin found that the sexual drought is equally common in marriages with stay-at-home mothers, a finding that reveals a deeper, more fundamental truth: Maintaining a passionate connection with your spouse is hard work, no matter what your personal circumstances. Every added stress or strain only compounds an already challenging problem.

Small wonder, then, that couples with breadwinning wives find it tough to sustain a lusty sex life. Not only do they have to overcome the considerable problems every couple faces, but they have the added challenge of feeling, as one woman put it, "androgynous." Because for so many of us, our attitudes and values are at least a generation behind, and our sexual identities are inextricably linked with how we define ourselves as men and women. Those definitions are blurred when there's a gender role shift.

Some couples find ways to make things work by clinging to some traditions. Barry made a lot of money as a TV writer when he and Anne were first dating, and he always treated Anne very extravagantly. When the TV work slowed down just as Anne's business picked up, it was a difficult adjustment for both of them. Anne took on all of the household and family expenses, but they naturally fell into an arrangement that suited both of them. "We go out every weekend, to make sure that we have some quality couple time," explains Anne. "Barry is responsible for planning and paying for date night. I feel taken care of, and I think it makes Barry feel good to be able to pick up the check for something."

Not surprisingly, when women make more money than their husbands, it can cut to the very core of both partners' sense of themselves as attractive, desirable, and sexually attuned. Couples have to reinterpret and reinvent the basic qualities of masculinity and femininity, but all of that is going to take us a while. It won't happen today or tomorrow. We're figuring it out as we go.

THE NAKED TRUTH ABOUT
GENDER ROLES

It's been said that there is no sex without sexism, and although we know that this is no longer true as equality becomes more and more the norm in relationships, it is hard to deny that sexuality is still closely tied to gender roles in people's minds. When women take over as the main provider and the basic notions of masculine and feminine are shaken loose from their traditional foundations, some of the mystery and intrigue of gender roles is lost. "When yin becomes yang, that sense of otherness disappears a little . . . and let's face it: Otherness is sexy," says Claire. But couples need to realize that yin and yang are never going to be the same no matter what role you fill in the family. That "otherness" is inherent in men's and women's biology and physiology, regardless of what each partner does for a living. The tautness, the tension between two individuals attempting to live a life together, the pull between independence and dependence, the need to be oneself rather than feeling controlled by the other . . . these conflicts are inherent in a love relationship—no matter who does the dishes—and give it that slight edgy feeling that is part and parcel of romance.

Many of the women we spoke with talked about the difficulty of shifting gears from their workplace personas as tough, capable, invulnerable warriors into their at-home roles, where they say they'd like to express the softer and more emotionally connected side of themselves. The problem creates a sort of gender-role whiplash, as women seesaw between two very different settings that demand sometimes diametrically opposed behavior.

"After a long day when I've had ten fights in the office and I've had to be as tough and competitive as my male colleagues, I go home with fangs," admits Sheila, forty-four, who manages a high-end mutual fund and is married to Patrick, a freelance journalist who also serves as the primary caretaker for their two adolescent children. Sheila says she has a long train ride home, which gives her some transition time, but often it's not enough. "I'll be nice to the kids but turn around and bite Patrick's head off. He'll say to me, 'Don't talk to me like that. I don't work for you,' and I'll realize I've been barking orders at him like a drill sergeant." Sheila's sense of helplessness and exhaustion causes her to strike out at Patrick.

"I know our role reversal is one of the reasons we don't have sex very often. I just don't feel particularly feminine most of the time, and I also get really tired. I have two speeds: hyperdrive and stop." But their role reversal itself is not the issue; rather, it's their attitudes and feelings about the role reversal that cause the problem. The hurt and resentment they feel toward each other build over time, making each of them withdraw emotionally and romantically.

Sheila and Patrick try to balance their sexual dry spells at home by taking three-week family vacations every winter, during which they reconnect romantically and sexually. "At a very basic level, our lives work, and so does our marriage," she says. "But we often function more as business partners than lovers. Thank God for those vacations. It's great to have a moment to take a deep breath and remember that Patrick isn't just the guy who takes out the trash and coaches the kids' soccer teams."

Making time for vacations away from your home routine and weekend getaways alone (without children) is important because it says to your spouse that you want and need to be together, that you desire each other. It's often hard to get away when children are small, but as they get a little older, seek out vacation spots for the whole family that offer day camps or special activities for children. This leaves time for you and your spouse to be alone, if only to take a walk together. And when you do get away, make a pact to leave problems and conflicts behind. What you need is a dose of positive energy.

While studies show that men's sex drives are less affected by the vicissitudes of their daily lives and emotions—they seem better able to put stress and worry aside for the sake of a steamy encounter—the role reversal can pose challenges for them as well. As we explained in chapter 1, when a woman takes over the provider role, it can deal a devastating blow to men's sense of masculinity—a situation that can create a sexual backlash of its own. Some men may have problems with impotence, a physical condition that often provides a mirror for how they're feeling emotionally. Others may lose interest in sex or try to assert their dominance in the bedroom. Still others might find solace for their wounded egos in someone else's bed—the ultimate sexual revenge.

Men are as confused as women by the new family paradigm. Frank Pittman, psychiatrist and family therapist, says in his book *Man Enough: Fathers, Sons and the Search for Masculinity,* "Men always know they are far less masculine than they think they should be. Women, though, have the power to give a man his masculinity or take it away, so women become terrifyingly important and terrifyingly dangerous to men." Women's exhaustion after a hard day's work (followed by a second shift taking care of kids and doing housework) often ends in sexual rejection of the man.

Pittman also talks about how men enter marriage under the happy assumption that they are about to enjoy a life of frequent sex. Unfortunately, their brides don't know this—and men don't realize that their brides aren't operating under the same assumptions. It's not that women don't enjoy sex. What happens in practice is that many women experience this expectation as a peculiar and sometimes exploitative demand. So when men are faced with the idea that they somehow have to be romantic, need to put women in the mood—and that even then sometimes women are just not interested—they are flummoxed. They really don't get it. There are many differences in the ways that men and women typically approach sex—differences that can easily create conflict. For example, most men have sex in order to feel close to their wives, whereas women need to feel connected before they have sex. Men also use sex to relieve stress. But if women are stressed, they need to calm down before they have sex.

Helen, thirty-one, a political lobbyist, has always made more money than her husband, Rob, forty-three, a high-school guidance counselor. She also is more driven, more organized, more "together," as she says. "He's very lovable and social," she says, "but there are times that I feel like his mother more than his wife—not a very sexy feeling." Although Helen has seen counselors off and on to talk about her frustration with the marriage, she didn't realize that Rob was having his own problems with their relationship until she began finding phone calls on their bill to a number she didn't know.

"I finally got curious one day, so I called it, and it was the mother of one of the students at his school—this sexy redhead," recalls Helen. "I had met her at a party several months before, and I'd thought she and Rob acted strange around each other. When I saw the phone calls, my heart sank. I was certain they were having an affair."

When she confronted Rob with the minor evidence she had, he confessed immediately—and blamed the infidelity on her. "It was awful," she says. "He said I made him feel like less than a man, that with every success I became more egotistical and distant. I admit that I hadn't been that interested in sex. I'd been so busy and involved with my career that sex fell way down on my list of priorities. But when I found out he was cheating, I was devastated."

Helen and Rob are trying to work things out in marital therapy for the sake of their three children, but she says it's slow going and there have been many times she's nearly left. "I'm proud of my success, but I feel like it's the worst thing for our marriage, and I don't know what to do about that," she says. "Am I supposed to give it all up just so he doesn't feel bad about himself, so he can feel macho and studly again?"

Adultery is terribly painful and can cause an irreparable breach in a marriage unless the wounded partner is able to fully understand and forgive. Women's careers don't create the problem. It's caused by years' worth of accumulated hurts and resentments toward each other. With effort, Helen and Rob will be able to resolve their difficulties—whether they remain together or part. Adultery invariably leads to tremendous damage in the relationship and, more often than not, to divorce. Rob would have been much better off insisting that he and Helen seek counseling, rather than acting on his temptation.

Not all reports we received from behind couples' closed doors were negative. When the wife becomes the chief breadwinner it doesn't automatically doom you to a sexless purgatory. In fact, some of the couples we spoke with said their sex lives were wonderful—even enlivened by their atypical financial roles. Some women said they relished the opportunity to shed their workplace leadership role and be the followers in bed. Others said their fiscal dominance carried over into the bedroom—with satisfying results. Meanwhile, certain men said they found their wives' powerful work roles highly erotic.

No one has ever conducted a scientific study of how sexuality changes when couples swap traditional roles, but in her book *Peer Marriage*, sociologist Pepper Schwartz found some evidence that sex is different in more egalitarian relationships. Her study showed that couples who share numerous roles—household as well as economic—use more positions and experiment more in bed, not because they're more sexually liberated but because they "have a relationship in which both partners have the power to suggest, innovate, and break out of role expectations." Couples can do this if they are friends and allies and if they can keep hostility to a minimum. Always try to view your partner in a positive light, keeping the good things in mind. Dwelling on the negative is self-indulgent and self-pitying and is bound to create a distance between the two of you. Validate each other, listen to each other, and have empathy for each other. You need to be friends and allies above all else.

THE LIBIDO KILLERS

"My sex drive was always high until I had children," says Claire, who says that she and her husband, Greg, have had sex about three times a month since they had their first child five years ago. "All of a sudden my workload increased dramatically. By the time I have the kids in bed at night all I want to do is curl up with a good book. I'll think about having sex, but it just seems like one more chore—another thing I *should* do. It's like I've lost sight of the fact that it's something I want to do, that it's actually fun and relaxing. My desire is buried underneath layer upon layer of stress."

Claire knows that her lack of interest in sex isn't caused by a physical problem, because when she and Greg go on vacation or have a night alone without the kids, her desire comes bounding back like a long-lost Labrador puppy. "It's reassuring to know it's still there, I guess," she says. "But it would be nice if I could feel that way on a regular basis, in the course of our day-to-day lives."

On the one hand, research shows that having children gives working women a mental and emotional boost that childless women lack. But kids also increase work and family strain. When scientists at Duke University measured working women's levels of the stress hormone cortisol over twenty-four-hours, they found that those with at least one child at home secreted consistently higher levels of the chemical, which has been associated with feelings of mental distress.

The reasons for working moms' stress are myriad, but they can be boiled down to this: They have too much to do in too little time. One study found that in families without children, men and women both work about sixty hours a week, including work around the house. But as soon as there is a child in the family, the total work-load escalates for women. In a family with three or more children, women typically spend ninety hours a week working (both professionally and at home), while men's hours stay steady at sixty. The result: Men can relax more easily at home, while women walk in the door and see hours of unpaid (often thankless) chores. Indeed, studies of stress hormones have shown that working women's levels are higher at home over the weekend than their husbands', even when they hold similarly demanding jobs. And when levels of cortisol rise, it causes a drop in testosterone, the hormone researchers believe fuels sex drive in both men and women.

Stress affects us psychologically as well as physically, making us distracted and irritable—another reason most women can't effortlessly shift gears from their frantic workday mode into a slower, more sensual mood. As marriage expert John Gottman says, we have "prerequisites for sexual intimacy": We want to feel relaxed yet energized (fatigue is another common drag on desire), worry-free and calm (the ticker tape of tomorrow's to-do list playing in your mind can make it almost impossible to feel romantic), and emotionally connected with our partners.

Says Gottman in *Why Marriages Succeed or Fail . . . and How You Can Make Yours Last:* "Boys learn to see sex either as pure pleasure disconnected from emotional commitment, or as a vehicle for getting close to a girl. . . . for many teenage boys and men, there are no emotional prerequisites for having sex because closeness is the goal, not the cause, of the sex act. In contrast, women by and large need to feel physical and emotional closeness and tenderness before wanting to have sex. Making love confirms intimacy rather than creates it for most women."

Nothing makes women feel less affectionate and loving toward their partners than feeling overwhelmed and underappreciated. When resentment builds, women often retreat emotionally and sexually, making sex a silent weapon in an unspoken (sometimes even unconscious) war. Romantic withdrawal is a perfectly passive way to wound your partner, who through his lack of participation around the house, through his lack of appreciation for your financial contributions, through his lack of awareness of your emotional needs, has, intentionally or not, hurt you.

"A lot of women out there are mad," notes the *Newsweek* cover story on sexless marriages. "They're mad that their husband couldn't find the babysitter's home number if his life depended on it. Mad that he would never think to pick up diapers or milk on his way home. Mad that he doesn't have to sing all the verses of "The Wheels on the Bus" while trying to blow-dry his hair. Those of us who were weaned on *Fear of Flying* or *Our Bodies, Ourselves* understand that we're responsible for our own orgasms. But then couldn't somebody else take responsibility for the laundry once in a while?"

The phenomenon is more acute in women with children, but it's not confined to them. Candace, the attorney we wrote about in chapter 2 who would like to cut back her hours to "be a wife," is childless. But she says it's still an effort to stay sexually connected to her lower-earning husband, Chip. "I love him dearly," she says, "and if I had it to do over again, I wouldn't choose to marry anyone else, but I feel like I spend half my life angry at him about something. He's so irresponsible about everything, from household chores to money, that I end up having to always be the responsible one. He's like a darling four-year-old, but I'm not going to have sex with a four-year-old."

After several years of "less and less frequent" sex, they discovered what she slyly refers to as "the joys of morning sex." "If we do it when we first wake up, he hasn't had time to piss me off. By the end of the day there are so many issues I feel angry about, sex is the last thing I want to do. But after a good night's sleep I'm able to let a lot of it go. I usually wake up in a good mood, so it's a nice way to start the day."

For working moms who are exhausted multitaskers and have an even greater need of their partners' help and support, the situation becomes exponentially more challenging. Most of the women we spoke with said they weren't necessarily looking for romantic gestures like scented candles and massage oil, although those touches are always nice. Rather, they said, it's what goes on outside the bedroom that has the potential to recharge or drain their desire.

"After we had kids I started seeing the inequities between what I do and what Greg does around the house," says Claire. "He'll leave his clothes lying on the floor or dirty dishes in the sink, and I'll clean up after him, fuming the whole time. Then he wants to be romantic. I feel more like kicking him than kissing him. I just wonder when he's going to realize that folding the laundry is the ultimate turn-on."

Indeed, Gottman's studies have shown that when husbands do their share around the house, both partners report a more satisfying sex life than in marriages where the wife believes her husband is a slacker. In *The Seven Principles for Making Marriage Work,* he says, "The quantity of the husband's housework is not necessarily a determining factor in the housework = sex equation. But two other variables are. The first is whether the husband does his chores without his wife having to ask (nag). A husband who does this earns enormous points in the emotional bank account. The other factor is whether he is flexible in his duties in response to her needs. For example, if he sees that she's especially tired one night, does he volunteer to wash the dishes even though it's her turn? This conveys the all-important honor and respect for her. Helping his wife in this way will turn her on more than any 'adults only' video."

Men need to realize—and if they don't, women need to tell them—that by taking charge of household responsibilities and doing chores without whining and without waiting to be told, they become sexier to their wives. In *Manhood in the Making: Cultural Concepts of Masculinity,* cultural anthropologist David Gilmore says, "Manhood's heroic quality lies in its self-direction and discipline, it's absolute self-reliance." A man (in a woman's eyes) takes loving care of his wife and children when he does what needs to be done to keep the family functioning, without resentment, and without waiting to be told. When he cleans up after himself simply because that's what a grown-up is supposed to do, his wife is going to get turned on. He'll see the difference in the bedroom.

Splitting housework and child care more equitably not only diminishes a woman's frustration but also can cut down on her fatigue, an underappreciated culprit in the desire dilemma—and one that seems to cut across gender. It's not only women but men who feel exhausted. In *How Tough Could It Be?,* his book about being a stay-at-home dad for six months, *Sports Illustrated* columnist Austin Murphy writes: "The truth is, since the start of the Experiment I have come to appreciate, more than at any other time in my life, the pleasures and advantages of retiring with a book before, say 9:30 P.M., and being asleep by 10:00. . . . To me, the most potent anti-aphrodisiac is what we shall call the Mom as Infinite Commodity Syndrome, where everyone needs a piece of my time or attention, so that at the end of the day, I've done nothing for myself."

REBUILDING A ROMANTIC RELATIONSHIP

There's an old joke that goes "How do you get a woman to stop having sex with you?" The answer: "Marry her." Irritatingly sexist though it is, it points out a disheartening truism about passion: It almost always wanes after your early courtship days, when the merest touch can send tingles to your groin. After that, you need to find ways—consciously and creatively—to keep the spark alive.

Trouble is, we've all been raised with an unrealistic myth: that good sex should be effortless. So that's the first idea to get rid of as you try to mend the broken links in your romantic connection. Both you and your partner need to be aware that married sex, no matter what your professional situation, takes work. In couples where women are financially dominant, that idea goes double.

Aside from the excitement of the new and unfamiliar, one of the key reasons early courtship is so passionate is because both partners are making an effort—they're engaged in the process of building a romantic relationship and invested in its outcome. As a result, they create a sort of sensual sanctuary—some couples call it a "bubble"—that provides a buffer from the daily stresses and strains of the world around them. They spend a lot of time holding hands, staring into each other's eyes, stroking each other's backs. They listen when their partner talks, laugh at his or her attempts at humor, respond to bids for attention with alacrity and enthusiasm.

As time goes by those nonsexual (but often sexually charged) interactions tend to fall by the wayside—to the detriment of your intimate connection and your sexual relationship. As a result, a relatively easy way to rekindle the flame of desire is to start behaving as if you and your spouse are still lovebirds. Walk arm in arm, kiss hello and good-bye, make romantic gestures part of your everyday physical vocabulary. Physical closeness can be a means to a healthy sex life, a stepping-stone that keeps sexual intimacy within reach, and it can be an end in itself, a way to connect on a romantic level without being overtly sexual. Sensuality is the name of the game.

At the same time, tune in to your spouse emotionally when you're together, or as Gottman says in *The Seven Principles for Making Marriage Work,* "Turn toward each other instead of away." "Watching Humphrey Bogart gather teary-eyed Ingrid Bergman into his arms may make your heart pound, but real-life romance is fueled by a far more humdrum approach to staying connected. . . . Comical as it may sound, romance actually grows when a couple are in the supermarket and the wife says, 'Are we out of bleach?' and the husband says, 'I don't know. Let me go get some just in case,' instead of shrugging apathetically."

Listen to each other; stay connected. When your husband laughs at an item in the newspaper, ask him what's so funny. When he looks irritated, ask him what's wrong. If you find yourself preoccupied with work, remind yourself to stop and be more present in the moment. If necessary, allocate ten minutes every day to think about your work problems but explain to your spouse that this is what you are doing. It may help to write down problems and possible solutions during this time. Then put the notebook away in a drawer—a concrete gesture that can symbolize putting your worries and concerns aside.

While you're reestablishing a physical and emotional connection, evaluate how much time you and your spouse actually spend alone together. Whether out of guilt or a heartfelt belief that they need to spend more time with their children, many of the couples we spoke with compensate for putting their children in day care by eliminating any extracurricular activities that don't include the whole family. This sounds like a noble impulse until you realize that it means couples are sacrificing a key component of a happy marriage and, not coincidentally, a good sex life: companionship.

Says Leah, the litigator: "We get so little time together as a family that I feel guilty if I hire a babysitter so Frank and I can go out. I know it's silly—and maybe even unhealthy. But there's not enough time to do everything I want to do."

You've undoubtedly heard a million times that it can help to schedule a date night every week or two so you can get out without the children, but it bears repeating here: Spending time alone is critical to reconnecting as men and women, sexual beings with adult interests and needs. Have dinner out with friends; get tickets to a movie, a concert, or a show. Humor is essential. Force yourself to do some of these things. After you do, you will see that your children have not been damaged or emotionally scarred when you leave them for an evening out. You will feel reassured, so that should make the next time easier.

That said, carving out couple time can be tricky when there are so many other exigencies in your daily existence. It may help you bump couple time up on the priority list if you realize that maintaining a passionate connection isn't just important for you as a couple; it's important for the whole family. As Valerie Davis Raskin, M.D., writes in her book *Great Sex for Moms: Ten Steps to Nurturing Passion While Raising Kids,* "Intimate parents are more resilient, more affectionate, more peace-minded and forgiving. Intimate couples function better as a team, and that's good for kids."

Every couple's sexual needs are different, and they differ day to day, week to week, depending on what's happening in their lives. Sex doesn't happen in a vacuum, and it's not realistic to expect it to. But what is consistent, especially when the woman is bringing home more money, is that she wants to feel attractive and desired. Some of that can come through loving gestures—flowers, e-mails, phone calls during the day, a dinner out, a kiss on the neck. All of that goes a long way with women (and doesn't cost very much). Husbands who plan outings for the couple also score lots of points.

In general, both men and women, but especially women, feel more sexually receptive when their spouses are physically affectionate, considerate, attentive, interested and respectful. And, especially in our overscheduled lives, it's important for both men and women to have time alone, to reconnect with their own sexuality and sensuality. Dr. Raskin recommends scheduling "sensuality recharging days," during which you see a sexy R-rated movie in the afternoon, shop for a silky camisole and wear it that night, go to the library and read some erotic literature, take an early-evening nap, or write down the details of a particularly steamy sexual encounter between you and your spouse. The idea: to coax your buried sexuality out of the dusty back rooms of your consciousness and into the fore. Apply the same awareness to lovemaking, especially if it's become dull and predictable. Ask your spouse what he enjoys and tell him what you like. Take the time and effort to try a new position or make love in an unusual location.

In Frank Pittman's book *Grow Up! How Taking Responsibility*

Can Make You a Happy Adult, he writes: "Sex is good for you and good for marriage. For your sake I hope it is the one thing you do only with your marriage partner. Couples should do it regularly whether they want to or not. If there is a conflict about sex, they should do it as often as the more sexually eager partner wants it, but in the manner that the less excited one finds most agreeable. Foreplay should start the day before." And don't forget to put a lock on your bedroom door. You don't need to feel embarrassed in front of your children, nor do you have to explain it. Kids need to know that parents are entitled to private time.

Even with your best efforts, there are going to be times when one of you isn't interested in sex at all. That's fine, but do make the effort to take the sting out of the rejection. Psychologist and sexuality expert Lonnie Barbach suggests that couples talk about sexual interest in terms of a nine-point scale, with nine being extremely horny and one indicating you're about as eager to make love as to have a pap smear. The scale can help you communicate your interest or lack thereof without making it seem like a personal rejection. Even after years of marriage, being turned down can still be hurtful. You can't feel sexual all the time, but you can always be considerate of your partner—and consideration, practiced consistently over years of marriage—can be a powerful aphrodisiac.

The Keeper of the
Purse Strings

When Anne, the small-business owner, met Barry, the playwright, eight years ago, he had just sold a concept for a television show to Hollywood. Shortly thereafter, he sold a screenplay and another TV concept, and his career seemed poised for the big time. Anne, meanwhile, won several lucrative clients. "Things seemed to be going so well," she says. "From that first, stellar year, we bought our apartment in New York." They got pregnant within a year, and while Anne wasn't thrilled to be working eight- to ten-hour days when she had a young baby, she viewed it as tiding them over. "I thought it was temporary, just until Barry really established himself," she says.

Since that "first, stellar year," however, Barry has written prolifically and sold very little—a fact that is frustrating to her and demoralizing to him. "It's really hard on him, because he always gets great feedback but he hasn't had any big sales," she says. "He's always just a heartbeat away from a huge contract. He finds it very difficult to talk about with me, because everything I say sounds like a criticism to him."

And she admits she *is* critical—not of his work ethic so much as his cavalier attitude toward their finances. "When we first got married, we had a joint bank account, and it was a disaster," she says. "He's really irresponsible with money. For instance, he didn't pay his taxes, and kept ignoring warning letters from the IRS, so they froze our bank account. It was pretty awful." Since that early experiment with merging money, they've had separate accounts, but over the past few years of his work drought, Barry's has run dry. "His family sends him some money periodically, and he would have occasional writing gigs, but by last year I had to keep writing him checks," she says. "It was terrible for both of us. I'd ask him if he'd run out of money, and he'd admit that he had. Then I'd get out my checkbook."

What makes the situation more annoying, she says, is the fact that he still spends money as if he had it. "He thinks nothing of eating every meal out, or dropping a hundred dollars at the record store every week or so," says Anne, sounding exasperated. "Finally last year I told him he needs to make enough money to cover his own expenses. I don't think it's fair that I'm the one earning all the money and he seems to be reaping all the benefits."

Because of her resentment, Anne admits she has used her financial clout in their relationship to her advantage. When she was pregnant with their second child, she had their apartment renovated—over Barry's objections—because she wanted to add a third bedroom. As a result of the renovation, Barry's home office was reduced in size and was uninhabitable for months. "Even though he'd been renting an office out of the home for several months before we began work, he was really ticked off, and I guess I don't blame him," she says. "The truth is, if he had been paying the mortgage, or been paying for the renovation, his office probably wouldn't have been affected. But it was the most logical thing to do, and I was paying for it, so I felt like I was in charge."

It's been said that money—who makes it, who spends it, and on what—is the number one source of conflict in relationships. According to the Association of Bridal Consultants, more than 67 percent of newlyweds say the most serious argument in their first year of marriage is about money—and those are couples who are in the gaga phase of their relationship.

Why are finances such a lightning rod in marriage? How does the nature of the discord change when women outearn their husbands? And how do these couples find ways to smooth out fiscal friction and create monetary harmony—or at least a reasonable facsimile—in their marriages?

THE MEANING OF MONEY

Money is power, or so the saying goes. And in the past, it certainly seems to have been so. A study by British sociologist Jan Pahl found that in traditional relationships in which the husband's salary is preeminent, women tend to manage the meat and potatoes of household budgets—paying the bills, buying the groceries and school supplies—while the more global and weighty decisions about how money is allocated, whether it be to savings accounts, say, or stocks or discretionary spending, are usually made by the man.

Part of men's traditional fiscal dominance has to do with the fact that they were usually the ones making the money and, therefore, had final say over how it was spent. In the families described in this book, the tables have turned. Yet in our interviews, we found that women with bigger paychecks didn't automatically assume the patriarchal power role. Some rejected it consciously, based on a genuine desire for shared power and joint decision making. Others seemed to act more instinctively, motivated perhaps by a desire for more traditional at-home roles or a fear of money and all it entails.

Indeed, our cultural and family upbringing can influence whether we embrace financial responsibility or run headlong from it, no matter how successful we are at work. Even today, parents tend to emphasize to young boys the importance of earning money and being financially independent, while many young girls hear precious little on the subject. As a result, some women, even high-earning ones, are leery of money and the power it gives them. After all, it wasn't so long ago that money was considered too complicated and stressful a subject for female minds.

"Clay handles all of our day-to-day money and keeps track of our investments," says Sarah of her stay-at-home husband. "When I run out, I ask him for more. It's fine with me, because I don't like dealing with money. The only stumbling block is that he is more frugal than I am. He's the type who will go to Trader Joe's to get cheaper cereal and Target to get the least expensive paper towels. I'm not like that, and he sometimes balks at my spending."

Jill, who is married to Johnny, a stay-at-home dad, describes a similar situation. "If Johnny died, I wouldn't even know where to start with our finances," she says. "When we go out I don't take my wallet. He always has the money and the credit cards. I don't even know how much our mortgage is!"

Although Sarah and Jill profess to being hopeless money managers, the ceding of financial responsibility to their husbands may have a deeper cause: They may be compensating for their guilt about their powerhouse jobs. By handing their husbands full financial control—in effect handing them back a sense of mastery and masculinity—they're restoring a more traditional balance to the relationship. Even deeper is that sneaky old wish to be taken care of. As Colette Dowling states in *The Cinderella Complex,* we give up something of ourselves when we marry, and that something often seems to be related to autonomy and independence. Of course, mutual dependence in a marriage is normal and necessary. A man and a woman should both feel free to depend on each other; if they can't, why marry in the first place? So we're talking about a matter of degrees. It's this "little woman" need of ours that can make for the trouble—leading us to be completely dependent on a man to make financial decisions (as many of our mothers were), or looking to our husbands to give us permission to make our own financial decisions.

Even if your partner really knows what he's doing and is completely trustworthy, it's wise to stay on top of your finances, because the reality is, something could happen to him or your marriage. It's important that you have at least a minimum level of familiarity with your accounts and investments should disaster strike. An even greater danger is turning your money over to a man who is a terrible financial planner (sexy and loving though he may be). If this describes your mate, don't criticize and don't complain. Just accept what you've got and take the reins.

Men and women often have different relationships with money anyway—a situation that can create confusion when couples suddenly find themselves sharing a bank account or planning for retirement. In women, money is often more closely tied to emotion. A 2000 study conducted by researchers at Iowa State University found that more women than men consider shopping an "event," rather than a chore and that women are more impulsive in their purchases.

These findings reveal a deeper issue: Shopping isn't always about the things money can buy; it's about meeting our emotional needs—reducing fear, calming anxiety, feeling safe, and satisfying unmet desires for gratification and love. (They don't call it retail therapy for nothing.) Other women, like their male counterparts, enjoy the power and independence that moneymaking gives them.

Many women want the power to use their money in ways that they feel are essential to them, particularly in regard to the care of their children. Working women know how important educational opportunities were for them. They want to be sure that their children have the same opportunities they did, if not more. For many women, as far as their children are concerned, money is simply no object.

As a result, when couples clash over spending, their arguments are often about more profound issues than the price of the new loveseat, say, or the remodeled kitchen. They're about our sense of security, our unfulfilled needs, and our desire for autonomy, individualism, and freedom of choice—desires that may be especially acute in both men and women who are pioneering this new family structure. That's why strict rules on budgeting and money management don't work too well. Flexibility is key here. Each couple is different.

When men and women marry, they bring more than their individual earning power to the altar; they bring an invisible dowry of unspoken expectations. If your spouse is intent on squirreling away every dime to buy a house but you're more in the live-in-the-moment and buy-the-latest-clothes mind-set, you're bound to get battered on the shoals of financial conflict at some point—unless you learn to communicate your thoughts effectively.

Because money is often symbolic of emotional needs or expectations, the amount you earn or have in the bank is often beside the point. We found that even comfortably well-off couples have conflicts about spending. When money is tight, however, the challenges are even greater, because it can decrease both partners' sense of security, autonomy, and control over their own destiny, ratcheting up the stress level in the relationship and making every purchase a potential trigger for angry recriminations.

POWER STRUGGLES AND
HOW TO GET PAST THEM

While money has traditionally been tied to marital power, the whole construct becomes more complicated when women are the primary breadwinners. Some men, unaccustomed to being "subordinate" to women and feeling a lot of hidden shame about it as well, may assert their power in other ways. And some women may follow in their patriarch fathers' footsteps, laying claim to the control that has traditionally been a provider's due.

In our interviews, we identified a number of different types of power struggles; among these, five emerged as the most common. In the rest of this section, we'll explain the variations and offer advice on how to restore a sense of balance and marital unity.

The Patriarch in Pumps

Leigh, the commercial actress we introduced in chapter 3, is a spender. "I love clothes, and I always want the newest things in the stores," she says. "I also like my house to be nicely furnished, and I spend a fair amount of money on beauty maintenance, like hair highlights and manicures. The way I see it, money is there to be spent."

Austin, on the other hand, is more of a saver. For instance, he fought Leigh when she wanted to move from their twelve-hundred-square-foot home to a much more expensive one that was almost

triple the size. The fact that they now live in the home Leigh cov-
eted is probably directly related to the fact that she not only earns
far more money than Austin, but that as a result she feels entitled to
enjoy the fruits of her labor. With her larger paycheck comes com-
mensurate power—power she's willing to wield if it's the only way
she can get what she wants.

Not surprisingly, the couple clashed when, two years ago, they
finally merged their bank accounts after seven years of marriage.
"Austin would call me and say, 'Oh my God! You're spending so
much. How are we ever going to save anything?' " she recalls. "It was
difficult to hear that from him, because I thought, 'I'm making three
times as much money as you are. Who do you think you are telling
me not to spend it?'"

Meanwhile, Austin had a big-ticket dream of his own: to join the
local country club. But Leigh said no. "It costs ten thousand dollars
a year, and I thought that was an awful lot of money," she says.

Leigh isn't unlike the patriarchs of old who believed that their
paychecks entitled them to certain privileges and perks—namely,
being able to make most of the discretionary-spending decisions.
But Austin wasn't going to roll over and play dead. As a result, their
finances, which were pooled, had become a tug-of-war—one that
came to a head recently when Austin announced that he wanted to
move from their home in Florida to Illinois to be near his family.
"That really shocked me," Leigh says. "He actually wants both of us
to give up our jobs and start over. I definitely don't want to leave,
because all of my family is here."

Austin's bid to move sparked some heated conversations that ultimately softened Leigh's attitude. Partly to calm Austin's we-have-
to-move fever and partly because she recognizes that she does spend
too much money sometimes, Leigh has started limiting her shopping. "I'm really trying to focus more on saving than spending," she

says. "That's made Austin happier." At the same time, she acquiesced on the country-club membership.

"If that's what it takes to keep him happy living here, then I guess it's really worth it," she says. "It's something we'll probably both have fun with." Even though Leigh makes most of the money, she's come to realize the hard way that big decisions require not only both people's input but compromise as well.

The Nickel-and-Dimer

Power and dominance aren't always so obvious. Some couples make big financial decisions together and seem to be simpatico when it comes to spending. But underneath the placid surface there's a subtle control issue at work that can cause tension and resentment.

Eliza, thirty-eight, an accountant who makes half a million dollars a year and has five children, is married to Vince, also thirty-eight, who was laid off from his high-tech job three years ago and has been a stay-at-home dad ever since. "We knew in college that math wasn't his thing, so I take care of all the money," she says. "He has full access to it, though. He'll call me and say, 'Write down that I'm taking forty dollars out of the bank.'"

Although she says that "neither one of us is into power plays," she admits that she's very, very frugal—to the point of pushing her husband to clip coupons. "He hates to do it, but I really think he should," she says. "I earn a lot of money, but I have to work hard for it. I don't want to squander it."

Her husband, she says, has never been a big spender, but he doesn't have her miser mentality, either. She says she's "teaching him" to adopt her thrifty ways. "He called me recently from the sports store, because he was so proud he'd gotten twenty dollars off a pair of snowboarding boots. I really praised him for that. Sure it's only twenty dollars, but if you save twenty dollars here and twenty dollars there, it starts adding up."

Because Eliza said her husband wouldn't be comfortable talking to us, we don't know how he feels about being asked to clip coupons and find the least expensive snowboarding boots when he's staying home with five children. But for many men that would be a recipe for frustration, rancor, and ill will.

Both partners come into marriage influenced by their own family history, and in each family, money has different meanings—whether it's associated with control, security, safety, independence, opportunities for growth and change, or something else entirely. Some men and women were brought up in luxury, never having to worry about the value of money, and continue to behave that way even when their financial circumstances have changed considerably. Others may feel that money is the only thing they possess that makes them feel special; in that case they tend not to give it away unless it enhances their own self-esteem, nor do they spend money easily except on themselves. Still others are brought up in poverty and never forget it; they are angry and envious if they are married to someone who was brought up in some comfort. These may turn out to be the mean-spirited Scrooge types. Other people are so nervous and edgy that they overspend in an attempt to calm themselves, or they obsessively cut coupons in an effort to exert some control over their inner world. If one partner in a couple is suffering from any of these extreme relationships with money, then the other partner is in for trouble. These patterns don't shift without serious effort, usually involving candid discussions and deep soul searching. Enlisting the help of a therapist who specializes in financial issues could go a long way toward easing money-related stress.

Husbands Who Pull Financial Punches

Men's spending habits may be an even greater source of tension than women's. Lisa, whose husband, Timothy, is the stay-at-home dad who used to be a stock trader, says they have a joint account and their spending styles usually jibe fairly well. But when Timothy bought a $100,000 boat last year without consulting her, she was stunned. "It really rocked me," she admits. Even so, she didn't confront him about it. "At the time it didn't seem to be worth arguing about—I mean, we had the money. My friends were completely freaked out. They kept telling me to say something to him about it, but I didn't."

Lisa rationalizes her silence on the subject by saying "It's not like he does it all the time" and pointing out that she often spends "more than I should" on clothes for their children and shoes for herself. "He doesn't criticize me and question my spending," she says.

Lisa is probably more forgiving than most, willing to look the other way because Timothy's huge purchase doesn't affect her or their children—nobody has to make sacrifices in exchange for the boat. As for Timothy, this could be a one-time incident resulting from overenthusiasm, or it could be a sign of something new and foreboding on the horizon—possibly signaling boredom, loneliness, or unhappiness. As one husband says: "It's safer to sail a boat than to find a mistress." At the very least, Timothy's actions were disrespectful; in a marriage of equals, all big-ticket items should be discussed by both partners. Even if finances are completely separate, if a big financial decision will impact the other partner (and most major financial decisions will, unless funds are unlimited), an open discussion needs to happen first. Because Lisa truly isn't angry, she's in the perfect position to open the door to discussion with Timothy, simply by asking him why he bought the boat without first discussing it with her. She might ask him how he would have felt if she'd done something similarly extravagant. This kind of conversation could lay the groundwork for sounder—and more collaborative—financial decisions in the future.

The Myth of 50/50 Fairness

When both partners work, even if the wife makes more, some couples adopt an egalitarianism-or-bust mentality by trying to split the bills and household expenses right down the middle. But insisting on total financial equity can set up a less-than-loving dynamic, as Marcy, thirty-five, a personal trainer, reveals. Even though she earns 50 percent more than her husband, Ted, a teacher, she believes that striving for a 50/50 split is "fair." "We keep our finances separate," she says. "He pays half the mortgage, and I pay half. We try to share most expenses evenly."

She sounds happy with the arrangement, but once she starts talking about how it really works, it's clear that it doesn't foster a sense of sharing or support. When they go out for dinner, for instance, they try to take turns paying, but the approach can put a damper on the evening. "We used to be a little more tit-for-tat. He'd say, 'I paid last time, so it's your turn.' We've let that go a little bit because it can make things tense. It becomes more about money than the good time. I don't want that. There are couples who go to their graves bickering about the same dumb things all the time."

With big-ticket items, there's even more serious potential for conflict. "Right now Ted wants to buy a new truck, but he can't afford it," she says. "I'm sure he'd like me to help him out—and I have the money to do it, but I'm not going to. If it were more important, I would, but I want to push him to do it himself. My feeling is that if he wants something, he should plan a little better and go for it."

She pauses, then adds, "It's a little tricky because I'm going to need a new car soon, and I have enough in savings to buy one outright. I'm hoping he'll be able to buy his truck at the same time, so it's not completely awkward."

This is a tricky situation. In certain cases, giving somebody money who could easily earn it could be considered enabling behavior—sending the message "I don't think you can do this your-self, so I'm doing it for you." So if Ted was just lazy or disorganized, or incapable of saving, Marcy would be justified in witholding money from him. In other cases, Marcy and Ted's, for example—where it is understood that his income will always be limited based on his career path—it would be an act of generosity for Marcy to chip in on the new truck. It's not mandatory, but it would probably earn her a lot of goodwill in the relationship.

The 50/50 split on expenses is not necessarily a fair one when one partner dramatically outearns the other, because it means that the bigger breadwinner will always have more expendable income. A friendlier solution might be to divide expenses more in proportion to their income. Men who make far less than their wives but are forced to split bills evenly may become secretly angry, and that anger is bound to emerge in a different arena of their lives.

The Money-Versus-Dreams Dilemma

Rose, the screenwriter, and Mason, who works with disadvantaged youth, have similar spending styles and values about money. "We're not big spenders and we're not big hoarders," she says. "We defi-nitely feel strongly about saving for college and that sort of thing, but we also like to enjoy nice meals out and fun vacations."

The problem for them is that Rose, like Anne, feels strangely dis-empowered by her breadwinner role, because her husband gets to follow his professional dreams while she carries the responsibility of paying the bills. Rose was happy to support Mason through graduate school, but when he took low-paying job after low-paying job after he graduated, she began to feel taken advantage of. "It suddenly dawned on me that my husband has the luxury of being a purist," she says. "He can do a job he loves but that brings in little money because I bear the brunt of the financial responsibility. When we fight about it he says, 'You knew this was what I wanted to do,' and I say, 'Yeah, but I didn't think you'd want to do it forever.' "

Many women in Rose's position are angry and bitter. They feel exploited. They are working too hard, carrying the brunt of the financial responsibilities, feeling exhausted—and watching their spouses enjoy life more than they are. It's a matter of fairness. If the balance has shifted so much that Rose is feeling unduly burdened, then Mason has to step up to the plate. It doesn't mean that he necessarily has to change his career, but he has to figure out a contribution that Rose will value and appreciate—something that will enable her to enjoy her life more. Maybe it's helping out more with the family or taking on additional housework that would ease the burden for Rose. Mason's justification—that Rose always knew about his plans—goes only so far, because none of us can anticipate how our needs will change as responsibilities grow. Rose needs to articulate this in a way that doesn't disparage or devalue Mason's work. She should also offer suggestions for things that he could do that would make her feel less resentful and stressed-out, and more satisfied with her own life. They'll both need to be flexible and open to change. Sometimes marital counseling can help with this sort of negotiation. An objective professional outside the relationship can help communicate each partner's needs and position to the other without the emotional baggage that can make similar conversations at home too heated.

YOURS, MINE, AND OURS:
THE MANY ROADS TO FISCAL BLISS

The good news? In our interviews, many couples said that money isn't a big point of contention in their marriages for one simple reason: Most female breadwinners have chosen not to exercise the power that can come with a larger paycheck, opting instead for a team approach that puts them on an even footing with their spouses and allows their husbands to retain a critical sense of power and influence.

For very traditional men, like Duane, the insurance adjuster we profiled in chapter 1, their wives' attitude can literally make or break their marital happiness. "If I had a wife who flaunted the fact that she makes more, that would bother me a lot. I'm not sure I'd make it with someone like that. But Ruth doesn't do that, even though she's the banker in our house. She takes the attitude that all the money that comes in is our money."

The concept of "our" money seems to be one key for these couples who avoid financial strife, but that doesn't necessarily mean having a joint account and putting everything into a communal pot. Rather, it's an all-for-one-and-one-for-all mentality that suffuses their interactions and girds their decision-making process—and makes them feel like true partners.

Frank, the stay-at-home dad who is married to Leah, the litigator, says, "We're very like-minded financially. We're not big spenders, but we do nice things, like rent a house on Maui every year. We try to make financial decisions together. It's not always easy. But we know we're in this for the long haul, so we're motivated to keep talking and work through things."

Sandy, the magazine editor who is married to Ben, the sculptor, says that she's aware of the fact that her earning power could give her financial dominance, but she has never used it that way. "If we want to make a big purchase," she says, "we talk about it. But we don't put too much pressure on each other over the little things. If he wants a sweater, he'll buy one. We look at our relationship as a partnership. We never did his money, her money. Early on in our marriage he inherited a chunk of money, and it went into the communal pot."

Couples who have similar spending styles and attitudes toward money will have an easier time making the financial aspect of their relationship work. Likewise, couples for whom money is plentiful have fewer conflicts. But even couples with disparate approaches and tight finances can find ways to mesh. Veronica and Tony, both forty-five, met when they were college freshmen and idealistic artists. They dated on and off throughout college and moved together to New York when they graduated. But after several years they started having problems, because she had taken a job in advertising and started working seventy to eighty hours a week. "He'd fallen in love with a bohemian artist, and I was turning into this workaholic," she says. "We had lots of arguments about how much I'd changed. I loved my job, though, and had no intention of giving it up for him." They eventually split up but remained friends, seeing each other every couple of months even as they drifted in and out of serious relationships with other people.

Finally, ten years after they broke up they "started moving toward each other again." They were married within twenty months. Because he was still a "struggling artist" she footed the thirty-five-thousand-dollar bill for their wedding. "He didn't have a problem with me making more money, but we did have to figure out our boundaries around money, because we have very different approaches," she says. "He's by nature extremely frugal, and I'm much more profligate. It helped that we'd been friends for so many years, so we knew each other well and could talk about sensitive issues, but even so we had to work out some glitches. We decided we couldn't have a joint checking account because I didn't want to get into a situation where he was asking why I spent so much on a sweater or a pair of shoes."

Although his paychecks come sporadically, he pays many of their household expenses and handles the car payment. "When his savings are down he'll come to me and say, 'I need some money,' and I'll write him a check. He rarely asks for money for anything other than basic living expenses, but I wouldn't care if he had to. Our approach might not work for a lot of people, but it does for us."

When money is tight it can add a degree of tension to the relationship that couples with plenty of money don't have. Handling money crunches requires flexibility and a willingness to adapt to the changing circumstances, as Sandy and Ben found. "We've always been very frugal, and being the sole breadwinner made Sandy very anxious sometimes," Ben says. "We drove a Saturn station wagon for ten years, while all our friends were running around in Mercedeses and Volvos. We'd plan a vacation, then scale it back. When she'd start getting really anxious we'd talk about it and decide that maybe I should go back to work. But every time I'd start to dust off the résumé she would say forget it."

When Sandy was at "maximum anxiety" about their finances, Ben says he'd beat himself up a little bit for not being the big breadwinner, but he never felt bad enough or guilty enough to be strongly disposed to make a change—until recently. "We knew we'd reached the point where we needed more income when we were facing college expenses. Our kids are in high school, and we're starting to feel more squeezed with that big expense right around the corner. She brought up the idea of my going back to work, and I know that wasn't easy for her. Those conversations are difficult for both of us. Big changes are never easy."

Fortunately, right about the time they decided he should start looking for work, he received a call from a company looking for a copy editor, the position he had held years before. "I felt like Rip Van Winkle going back to work after ten years," he says. "Nobody has secretaries, nobody has stationery, everyone uses computers. It's been a big lifestyle change, and I miss being around for the kids and having time to work artistically. But, with the kids older, we'd gotten to a point where we knew it was possible for me to be out of the house for eight hours a day, and we need the extra income more than a body at home."

After interviewing couples at length about the ins and outs of their financial planning, we came to realize that there are no fast rules as to the logistics of how you keep your money, whether it's in a joint account, separate accounts, or the three-account system, in which the couple has a joint account plus each partner has his or her own account. Every couple faces different expenses—mortgage or rent, insurance, health care, utilities, car expenses, entertainment, and possibly kids' stuff—so the best way to handle it is by jointly creating a list of all of the monthly and annual expenses and together deciding who will pay for what.

Each couple is different and each couple has to find their own way, but there has to be a plan, whether it's formally negotiated or casually evolved, and both partners have to know what the plan is and what their responsibilities are. In some cases, one partner is a more reliable bill payer/record keeper and that person is responsible for handling all of the bills while the other is responsible only for providing his or her contribution (whether it's weekly, monthly, or annually). If you have the conversation once and establish the rules, you won't have to argue every time a bill comes in. This approach can also engender a sense of partnership, where you jointly determine what you might want to do with a surplus, should there be one.

There are practical points to consider when deciding which route to take. A joint bank account and joint credit cards can be handy, for instance, but the approach doesn't afford much privacy—every gift you buy for your spouse, as well as frivolous expenditures, will come out of that account.

If you do go the joint-account-only route, you also need short-term and long-term goals and some concrete discussions about spending habits. And you both need to be good about record keeping so that you can always have a handle on the flow of funds in and out of the account.

Some couples prefer to keep everything separate and pay their agreed-upon expenses out of their own individual accounts. While separate accounts may give each partner a greater sense of freedom and autonomy, this approach can unintentionally undermine the sense of "ours."

The third option, the "yours, mine, and ours" approach, can work for couples who want some individual privacy but who like the feeling of having shared resources as well. With this approach, you each commit to contributing a certain amount or percent of income into the joint account, from which all joint household bills are paid. Then the personal accounts are used for personal expenses. If expenses other than household expenses are going to come out of the joint account, it's reasonable to expect that big purchases will be jointly discussed and decided upon. Most couples say it's not practical to debate every ten-dollar expenditure, but it may help to set a spending threshold, be it fifty dollars or five hundred dollars, over which you have to check in with the other person before you pull the trigger. Negotiate an agreement that's fair and mutually respectful. After all, marriage is about sharing. And equal sharing in the power and decision making is essential if you both want to feel loved and respected.

The issue of money is complex, because it represents the intersection of several conflicting (and sometimes not easily reconcilable) factors: love, emotion, and practical realities. Whether you're the type to surrender the checkbook or commandeer control, you need to be sure you and your spouse have a similar financial plan and, if you don't, that you raise the subject and discuss your financial goals, desires, fears, and expectations. Women are asking for partnership, and that includes economic partnership, no matter who brings home more money. There has to be a commitment to the marriage, a true desire to share your life no matter how many difficulties there are, because there is no marriage without some difficulties. There has to be friendship and, most important, a feeling of trust. Successfully managing your finances together requires honesty, communication, flexibility, compromise, and a good dose of love and patience—indeed, the very qualities that make for a good relationship.

SEVEN

Fast Forward: The Next Generation

S andy, the magazine editor, and Ben, the sculptor who recently returned to work after years of being a stay-at-home dad, have two sons in their teens. Ben was an early adopter of the SAHD role, working artistically (but rarely for pay) from their suburban home for the boys' entire childhood. Neither one of them regrets the choice to have him fill the at-home parent role, even though it put a strain on their finances to have only one income they could count on.

"I feel fortunate to have had a parent in the house all those years," says Sandy. "I think my kids benefited from seeing me work—they certainly don't think for one minute that women should be home cooking and cleaning—and I think they benefited from having all that time with Ben. They have a great relationship with him. It was good for them to have a male role model who was such a hands-on parent."

Now that the boys are older, Sandy says she's starting to notice the ways in which their family arrangement has shaped her sons' attitudes. "They're pretty enlightened, as teenage boys go," she says. "They have lots of friends, both male and female, and they see women as friends and equals. I think they understand that they have many choices in life—they can have careers, they can raise children—and that those choices aren't dictated strictly by gender. They've also learned that not every relationship has to look the same. They have friends whose mothers work and some who stay home. They've seen a pretty broad range of families. I'm curious how they'll decide to structure their own."

Sociologists and psychologists are curious, too. As more and more families find alternative ways to balance work and child rearing, researchers in a variety of fields are eagerly gathering data on how these modern units fare in terms of emotional health and parent-child relationships as well as kids' school achievement and personality traits.

With one third of married women in our country making more money than their husbands, one can't help but wonder what lessons our children are absorbing about male and female roles. But how do children actually form their gender identities? How much do parents influence their children's attitudes about being a boy or a girl? Is the new family paradigm likely to influence their ideas? And, most important, are there steps we can take to foster an egalitarian worldview in the next generation?

HOW CHILDREN DEVELOP
GENDER IDENTITIES

From the time a baby's birth is announced with a pink or blue bal-
loon, the newborn is surrounded by messages about gender. For the
most part, very young children seem blissfully unconscious of the
differences between the way people typically behave, but by around
two years of age, they begin to call themselves "girl" or "boy"—and
sort others around them into gender categories. Because their thinking isn't very sophisticated, they categorize people based on superficial characteristics—clothing, hair length, occupation, interests—
and have amusingly rigid attitudes toward who does what, based on
what they've been exposed to. For instance, a child who has seen
only female dentists might declare confidently, "Men can't be dentists," and adamantly refuse to give an inch on this position, even
when presented with evidence to the contrary. Interestingly, these
small arbiters of gender appropriateness still don't realize that their
own sex is fixed—that if they're born a boy, they're going to grow to
be a man, and if they're born a girl, they're going to become a
woman. They won't develop the notion of "gender constancy" until
about age five or six.

Although the nature-versus-nurture debate may never be defini-
tively resolved, some of the research proposes that a handful of the
developmental and behavioral differences that typically appear between young girls and boys are driven by their biology. For instance,
by age two, aggression begins to decline in girls but remains constant in boys—a tendency, experts say, that can be exacerbated by
harsh discipline. Likewise, while preschool-age boys are typically
found to be more aggressive and to "take up more space"—to be
louder and more physically active—than their female peers, girls at

that age are, on average, more verbal. Other equally important studies show that parents are tougher on boys than on girls from birth on—less sympathetic and empathic, for instance—a form of social conditioning that may contribute to the tendency for boys to become less emotionally open than girls as they grow older.

While there are undoubtedly some biologically driven behavior differences, most experts agree that cultural influences play a leading role in shaping boys' and girls' ideas about gender and, as a result, their individual behavior. As the American Academy of Pediatrics' child-care bible, *Caring for Your Baby and Young Child: Birth to Age 5,* observes, "Even if both parents work and share family responsibilities equally, your child will still find conventional male and female role models in television, magazines, books, billboards, and the families of friends and neighbors. Your daughter, for example, may be encouraged to play with dolls by advertisements, gifts from well-meaning relatives, and the approving comments of adults and other children. Boys, meanwhile, are generally guided away from dolls (though most enjoy them during the toddler years) in favor of more rough-and-tumble games and sports. The girl who likes to roughhouse is called a tomboy, but the boy who plays that way is called tough and assertive. Not surprisingly, children sense the approval and disapproval of these labels, and adjust their behavior accordingly." The end result: By the time most children enter kindergarten, their notions of their own masculinity and femininity are well on their way to becoming established.

There's further evidence that the emotional differences that characterize boys and girls may be influenced more by nurture than by nature. For instance, studies show that while preschoolers' facial expressions are equally revealing, by age five or six, boys' faces start to become more inscrutable, a distinction that typically remains in place throughout men's and women's lives. The tendency for boys to back away from emotional expression and girls to embrace it could be an artifact of biology, but a body of research seems to indicate otherwise. Studies of adults have shown that men and women experience emotions with equal intensity—their hurts and disappointments are every bit as painfully acute, their joys are as ecstatic. But men cloak their feelings behind a mask of stoicism (remember the Lone Ranger?) while women are more comfortable letting their feelings show.

Because our internal experiences are so similar, the factor that most likely drives this difference, say many researchers, is culture. Eli Newberger, M.D., author of *The Men They Will Become: The Nature and Nurture of Male Character,* attributes the different behavior to "a blizzard of signals, many of them unconsciously sent and unconsciously received," that are directed to boys and girls from infancy onward.

Movies, books, magazines, and relatives serve as guardrails, steering youngsters toward "acceptable" male and female behavior, but parents—even the most enlightened and sophisticated—may intentionally and unintentionally send their offspring messages that teach them to hew to their gender line. Indeed, a number of studies have identified gender-specific parenting practices—that mothers smile more at infant daughters than at sons; that moms show a wider range of emotions with their daughters during toddlerhood; that fathers use more emotional words when creating stories for their daughters than for their sons; that mothers discuss the feelings associated with an emotion with their daughters but try to show their sons the causes and consequences of their emotions. Even day-care staffers send separate signals, smiling more and behaving in a more physically affectionate way with girls. Feelings of vulnerability in boys are met with teasing and contempt; stoicism and toughness are encouraged. Remember John Wayne's admonition: "Real men don't cry."

The effects of such training are evident early on. Dr. New-berger writes: "By ages three to five, children themselves are already reporting their belief that males express anger more, and females express fear, sadness, and happiness more. Eventually this duality is firmly in place: Females believe (and observers agree) that they express emotions more intensely than males do—both positive emotions such as happiness or joy, and negative emotions such as shame, guilt or sadness, fear or nervousness." The exception is anger, which both men and women agree lies almost wholly in the province of males. One reason for this is that socially, an expression of anger in women is considered not only unacceptable but unseemly.

Biology comes into play at puberty, when boys begin producing ten to twenty times more testosterone than girls, while girls produce more serotonin, a neurotransmitter in the brain that some say may block aggressive behavior by counterbalancing the effects of testosterone. Dr. Newberger points out in his book that the effect of testosterone is evident in several behavior patterns typical of growing boys. "The search for activities, from sports to sex, in which the body builds up physical tension and then releases the tension climactically; relatively short attention spans as the boy moves from one activity or focus to another; and the tendency to explore the problem-solving tasks in any situation—often neglecting the accompanying emotional situation—and to lose interest and patience if the problem can't be solved fairly quickly" could all be considered testosterone-driven behaviors, he says.

Now, we all know gentle, passive boys and aggressive, active girls, so there's obviously more going on than meets the eye. Indeed, another key factor that helps shape a child's gender identity is temperament. Although studies show that about 50 percent of personality is dictated by genes—if your child tends to be shy, he's never going to turn into a party animal, for instance—the other half is molded by the environment: parents and siblings, school, community, media, and the ever-changing values and mores of society at large. In one telling study, researchers at the University of California at Berkeley found that in the 1970s, women in their twenties and thirties who became involved in the women's movement grew more assertive, autonomous, and flexible, probably because it challenged old notions of how women *should* behave and provided an impetus for them to become more independent and self-reliant. Clearly, we humans are shaped by a complex interplay of genes and environment, biology and experience. Our individual temperaments and perspectives are undoubtedly guided by physiological factors, but the culture we live in shapes our attitudes and ideas in subtle yet powerful ways. Indeed, when it comes to raising children with gender-neutral values, a growing body of research reveals the considerable impact of parents.

HOW THE NEW PARADIGM
AFFECTS KIDS

"I think mothers are more cautious with children than fathers," says Johnny, one of the stay-at-home dads we interviewed. "I find that when I'm at the park some moms look at me funny, because I'll let my kids venture onto the higher bars of the jungle gym or I'll push them as high as they want to go on the swings. I'm curious to see how that will affect our kids."

Even so, he says there are far more similarities than differences between his parenting style and that of his many female friends. "The differences are mostly superficial—I tend to bring less healthy snacks to the park than the moms do and that sort of thing," he says.

"I'm a little more permissive than some of the moms, but it's nothing too drastic."

Perhaps that's one reason neither of Johnny's daughters, now four and two, seems to be aware of the fact that their dad is filling a role more often played by women. "It's just so normal for them to have Dad at home, I don't think they've thought much about it," he says. But he believes the mere fact of his presence at home, and his wife Jill's high-powered job, will be a potent influence on his daughters. "I think—I *hope*—it will help them grow up to be nonjudgmental and open-minded, to live and let live. I hope they're interested in reading, sports, culture—that they have a broad range of interests that aren't dictated by gender. Because I'm a man in a nontraditional role, I'm hoping that I'm serving as a good role model for that kind of attitude."

Judging from the bulk of the data on working mothers and involved fathers, Johnny's wish may well come true. A number of studies suggest that children raised by hands-on fathers—those who are emotionally present and warm even when they're not home especially often, as well as those who do most of the child care—reap a number of benefits, not the least of which is a flexible attitude toward gender roles and a wider expression of emotion.

In one study, University of Michigan researcher Norma Radin looked at behavior among preschool children and found that those whose fathers were responsible for 40 percent or more of the child rearing were more likely to have friends of both sexes and exhibit fewer gender-stereotyped expectations of their friends than kids with less present, less engaged fathers. Likewise, when Radin studied male and female adolescents whose fathers had been very involved in their early upbringing, she found that they were more open-minded in their expectations for family life—they had more liberal attitudes toward men and women sharing parenting responsibilities and toward dual-earner marriages in general—than their peers with more removed fathers.

Other studies show that the amount of time dads spend in activities with their children isn't the critical factor; what's more important, researchers say, is the nature and quality of the father's involvement. When researchers at Morehead State University surveyed two thousand men and women between the ages of eighteen and twenty-two, they found that an emotionally close, warm relationship with their fathers helps boys develop egalitarian attitudes toward gender, while girls' egalitarian attitudes were shaped more by their fathers' personality than by their relationship. A nurturing, warm, and emotionally expressive male seems to be key here. In contrast, a cold, distant father can make children less secure and self-confident, less willing to try new things, and more emotionally aloof.

Studies of the families of SAHDs have turned up similarly encouraging results. Kyle Pruett, M.D., a clinical professor of psychiatry at the Yale Child Study Center and Medical School, followed eighteen families with SAHDs from the time their first child was about a year old till the children were eight and ten. During his assessment of the children at age four, Dr. Pruett made the following observation: "There were signs that these children as a group might be developing a resilience and flexibility in certain areas of their personality development, particularly in the ease with which they moved back and forth between feminine and masculine behavioral roles (not identities, but roles). While their peers were concentrating on joining the appropriate 'gender gang,' they were moving comfortably back and forth between gender groupings at day care, playgrounds and birthday parties."

By the time the children were on the cusp of adolescence, says Dr. Pruett, caretaking, whether it was focused on a family pet or a houseplant, had become a central focus of their daily lives. In his book, *Fatherneed: Why Father Care Is as Essential as Mother Care for Your Child,* he writes: "While each child's gender identity remained quite stable, a certain flexibility of gender role performance continued to make itself known. . . . It occurred to me during the eight-year follow-up that having a father and a mother devoted to the nurturing of a child was such a pervasive culture in these families that children identified early with nurturing itself as a valued, powerful skill and role and wanted to explore their own competence in this domain."

Indeed, most of the families we spoke with who have very involved fathers also have very involved mothers—one of the biggest advantages today's SAHDs have over the homemakers of yesteryear. "Jill had maternity leave when we had the kids," says Johnny, "so we were both home for the first couple of months, which was wonderful. And now that the kids are older, when she gets home from work she likes to take over the parenting duties, so I don't ever have to fight with her about it. Judging from some of the comments of my female friends who stay home with their kids, most male breadwinners don't behave that way." You could say that kids with hands-on fathers have two role models for nurturing, both mother and father, a bonus that, according to Dr. Pruett's study, has noticeable effects. He also observed in his most recent follow-up that, while most of the peers of the children in his study were in the boys-(or girls)-have-cooties stage, the children of SAHDs were more comfortable forming friendships with kids of both sexes.

While it appears that a present, compassionate father exerts a strong influence on children's attitudes and ability to articulate emotions, studies show that kids with moms in the workplace also learn valuable lessons. Researchers have found, for instance, that daughters of employed mothers are more likely to eschew traditional gender-role stereotypes and to desire careers of their own in adulthood than daughters with at-home moms.

Researchers at the University of Michigan found that sons and daughters of employed mothers have a more egalitarian attitude toward gender. In their study of four hundred midwestern families, they discovered that girls with employed mothers were more likely than girls whose mothers were full-time homemakers to say they believe that women could do the activities that are usually associated with men—fix a car, climb a mountain, or fly an airplane. Girls with fathers who were more involved in housework and child care were the most likely of all the children in the study to hold this view. For boys, however, their mothers' employment status was not related to their measure of women's competence to do "male" activities, but both sons and daughters of working mothers felt that men could do "female" activities, while those with full-time homemakers did not.

The researchers found that the benefits of working moms extended beyond gender-role attitudes. Daughters of employed mothers, they observed, were more likely to be assertive in school—to participate in class discussions, ask questions when instructions were unclear, and feel comfortable in leadership positions. They also were less inclined to misbehave in the classroom. In addition, they were found to be less shy and more independent and to have a higher sense of efficacy than daughters of stay-at-home moms. Boys of working mothers had higher academic scores, but their mothers' working status didn't seem to affect their social adjustment one way or the other.

If raising a child with an egalitarian attitude toward gender roles is your goal, it's a good idea to pay strict attention to what goes on between you and your spouse at home. For instance, how household chores are divvied up—who does the laundry, the cooking, and the cleaning—has been proven to have myriad effects on children.

When sociologists Scott Coltrane and Michele Adams of the University of California at Riverside recently examined data from the Child Development Supplement of the Panel Study of Income Dynamics, a national survey of more than thirty-five hundred children and their parents, they found some surprising benefits when dads clean, cook, and run household errands with their school-age children. Indeed, they reported that school-age children who do housework with their fathers are not only more likely to get along with their peers and have more friends, but they're also happier, more outgoing, and less likely than other kids to act up at school and disobey their teachers. In fact, the research shows that children, both boys and girls, who do chores with their fathers exhibit even more positive behaviors than when they do housework with their mothers. The five chores that helped kids most: washing dishes, cleaning the house, doing laundry, preparing meals, and running errands.

One of the keys to successful sharing of tasks between husbands and wives is their own belief in gender equality, Coltrane says, adding that men and women who believe that fathers should be involved are the most likely to share all kinds of household and child-care tasks. The most profound benefit of that approach: By modeling cooperative family partnerships, men help prepare male children to share family work when they become husbands and fathers.

As we've reported previously in this book, men have some catching up to do in this area. Most studies show that the majority of husbands don't pull their share of the household load, even when their wives make more money than they do. In order for more men to take on the role of housekeeper and nurturer, men will have to understand and value the benefits of being involved, and society will need to become more accommodating toward men who step outside their traditional provider roles. While options like paternity leave are still far from widespread and too often underutilized when they're available, they're certainly a step in the right direction. And there are other encouraging signs of a major shift in our cultural attitudes toward men as caretakers. Baby-changing tables are starting to appear in men's bathrooms in airports and some fast-food chains, and there are more and more play groups for at-home fathers and their children, according to the At-Home Father Network.

It's almost impossible to overstate the benefits of shared parenting and shared housework. Involved fathering has an impact on the relationship between spouses, which, in turn, has a positive trickle-down effect on children. Studies show that women who feel supported by their husbands in their child-rearing roles are more patient, flexible, and emotionally available to their children. And research by marriage guru John Gottman has shown that women interpret their husbands' domestic contributions as a sign of love and caring and are therefore more sexually attracted to their mates.

We tend to think of housework (and even some aspects of child care, to a certain extent) as trivial, but the cumulative amount of work we do in terms of maintaining our homes and caring for our children actually exceeds the number of hours we put in at work. Moreover, it helps shape our children's ideas of relationships, of fairness, of how men and women are supposed to behave. Trivial? We hope we've proven in this and the preceding chapters that what happens in our homes is anything but.

HOW TO RAISE KIDS WITH EGALITARIAN VALUES

The roles of fathers and mothers don't need to be identical in order to impart a sense of fairness and equality to children. Men and women are different, and we see no reason to pretend that isn't so. Men approach parenting in a slightly different way and often have their own ideas about how housework should be done. Learning to accept and respect their individual efforts is the first step toward bringing men back into the household fold and making them feel comfortable, wanted, and needed in this traditionally female domain.

By virtue of the fact that you've adopted a forward-thinking partnership, you're already offering your children an advantage: You've opened up their perspective to a new way of doing things. Now you need to be aware of the fact that the conscious and unconscious choices you make in your day-to-day lives can serve to undermine or support your child's open attitude toward domestic and economic roles. Talk to your partner about the values you want to impart to your children so you can determine what is important to both of you. Do you want your children to be open-minded? Self-reliant? Flexible in their attitudes toward gender roles? Nurturing and empathetic? What legacy would you like to leave for your children, and how do you think your lifestyle will contribute to that goal?

Examine your own attitudes and behaviors to see how you might be influencing your children without even knowing it. Do you think of yourself as the primary caretaker for your child, even though both you and your husband work? Studies have shown that parents who say the mother is the child's primary caretaker have more traditional sex-role attitudes when it comes to child rearing than people who say that both parents are the child's primary caretakers. Do you silently take up the slack around the house without expecting your husband to do his share? If so, it won't take your kids long to learn that women are "supposed to" do housework, even if you have a more high-powered career than your spouse. Being a role model means just modeling the behavior you want your kids to adopt.

Be very careful to remember that a part of your mind may be

stuck in a time warp. Encourage your sons to express their emotions and vulnerabilities. They won't turn into "sissies"; it actually takes courage and strength to be emotionally expressive and available. Don't overprotect your daughters. They need to be strong and self-reliant. Competitive sports are important for both genders. Teach all children to be assertive and free to express their opinions, and not to be afraid to be different. Girls as well as boys should be allowed to feel their anger, and both should learn to express it kindly. All children should be responsible for chores in the house, and when they're old enough, they should be given an allowance and taught to manage their own money.

Studies show that parents who are authoritative—who discipline their children with love and respect—tend to have kids with more fluid attitudes toward gender roles than those who are authoritarian, who have rigid behavioral expectations that are enforced with a "because I said so and I'm the mother/father" approach. The tone of your voice and the assuredness of your manner are what make all the difference. Behaving like a tyrant is never necessary or useful. It's all too easy for busy parents to become overly strict or overly lenient in their discipline. Neither style takes as much work as setting limits, holding your temper, explaining the rules in a way that kids understand and sticking by them. Setting high behavioral expectations for your children and guiding them gently and compassionately toward those goals seems to produce not only the most self-confident and socially adept kids but also the most open-minded and creative.

Think about how you're going to talk to your children about your family's gender-role choices, because it's a sure bet that at some point they're going to ask. Leah, the New York City litigator, was putting her six-year-old daughter to bed recently when her daughter asked, "Why do you have to work when lots of the other moms stay home?" Leah had to take a deep breath before answering. "This issue is hard for me, because I'm not entirely enchanted with being the breadwinner," she says. "But I explained to her that every family has to have money to pay their mortgage, buy food, and take vacations, which means that at least one parent needs to work. I didn't get into the whole gender issue, because I don't think she was asking why I work and Frank doesn't. She just wanted to know why I don't stay home, too."

Her daughter's question prompted a whole new round of mulling for Leah. What she came away with: Although she isn't certain she wants her daughters to emulate her breadwinner lifestyle, she is hopeful that by seeing her work they'll "learn to be self-reliant and to take care of themselves." To further that attitude, she has set up both girls with bank accounts and takes them periodically to make deposits. "That's not so different from what many other parents do," she says, "but I think it might carry more weight when the person who is telling them about the importance of being financially responsible is their mom, who also happens to be the family breadwinner."

RULES FOR THE NEXT PHASE

Men and women today face enormous challenges, living in a society that is becoming one of increasing gender equality, economically, socially, and politically. It's a time of great flux, and there are no obvious role models. Couples are searching in the dark and stumbling upon individual solutions that work for them.

When couples don't have children, the problems and conflicts in their marriages typically produce far less tension. In reality, an economic and domestic partnership helps both men and women.

When both partners work, they may feel more secure in an insecure economy. If one spouse loses a job, the other one can function as a safety net. Or if one wants to change careers or go back to school, the other can be relied on to hold the fort. When both members of a couple are working they have more funds and can save for a home and for future expenditures. Even so, household tasks have to be split between the two; flexibility and a willingness to negotiate are imperative if the marriage is to work. Fortunately, young couples today are much better at discussing and compromising than couples of their parents' generation.

We've come a long way in the transition toward fully realized gender equality, but there's still a distance to go. Here are some final pointers—the ten commandments, if you will—that will help you smooth the way for yourself and for the generations to follow:

1. Make mutual respect priority number one. If you and your spouse truly respect and support each other's choices, you'll both feel more secure in your lifestyle— and be well on the way to smoothing over some of the most difficult issues that crop up in role-reversal marriages. The reverse is true, too: Once contempt creeps into a relationship, it's downhill all the way.

2. Have reasonable expectations. Accept the fact that your marriage is not going to be happy at all times, because let's face it: It just doesn't work that way. Marriage is real life. A relationship takes tolerance, patience, and hard work—especially when you're pushing the bounds of tradition.

3. Be committed to the marriage. Don't throw around the word *divorce;* even empty threats are wounding to your partnership and can undermine trust in the relationship.

Both partners need to know that the other is in it for the long haul.

4. Negotiate differences. When conflicts arise, be sensitive to the partner for whom the issue is more important. Let his or her will prevail to the extent that it's possible and practical. Don't let resentments pile up. Talk about differences, misunderstandings, conflicting interests, irreconcilable schedules, and so forth, as soon as you can. If resentments get out of hand and communication breaks down, seek marital counseling right away.

5. Don't sweat the details. Keep in mind that your house may not look the same way your mother's or grandmother's did because your life is different from theirs. Accept the fact that certain chores may fall through the cracks—dust will gather, Cheerios will collect under the sofa, and laundry will most certainly pile up. You can't be perfect and you can never do it all, so figure out what your priorities are, who can handle what, and which chores or responsibilities can be postponed.

6. Invest in your relationship. Budget for a babysitter, and go out to an early movie and/or dinner one night a week or as often as you can. Tell your spouse you love him, and if he doesn't tell you, remind him that you need to hear those words, too. Never come home or leave the house without a hug and a kiss. Touch each other, hold hands—physical affection can help you create a haven of emotional closeness that offers some protection from the stress of the world.

7. Strive for balance. Both men and women need time with friends, a key to peace of mind, especially for women. When you're feeling strung out, take a breather: Exer-

cise, jog, do yoga, meditate, give each other a massage, put on music and dance, make love. Develop and indulge in hobbies or passions. You'll not only benefit personally but will set a strong, positive example for children by creating an environment in which learning is nurtured and encouraged.

8. Share the power. Children need to see that their parents are partners in all ways—domestic as well as economic. In SAHD households, it's important to make clear to children that Daddy, even if he stays at home, shares decision-making power in every way. Genuine partnership is key in households with or without children.

9. Keep your sense of humor. There's no more potent weapon against stress and resentment than laughter. It helps release physical tension and rebuild personal connection. Research has shown that humor is a powerful strategy for overcoming adversity in a marriage.

10. Celebrate your success. You and your spouse are forerunners in a revolutionary time, and the lives you create will serve as role models for generations to come. You're sure to have tough times, but the simple fact that you're on this path is an accomplishment in itself. Enjoy the journey.

As we move forward toward new gender goals, keep in mind that it's not necessary for men and women to become more androgynous—a word that connotes not so much a blurring of gender as a complete annihilation of it. Rather, the hope is that as the pioneers of the new family frontier become more vocal and visible in society, the tide of public opinion will gradually turn, bringing with it the richness, depth, and complexity this new paradigm promises—indeed, that is the hallmark of many couples we spoke with for this book. As more and more men feel emboldened to become nurturers, and women continue to express their professional creativity and ambition, couples will find new ways of relating to each other that transcend the traditional strictures of gender roles, without forsaking the underlying sexual tension and romantic connection at the core of a successful partnership.

In addition to following the strategies we've outlined here, you can and should create new ones that fit the unique needs of your situation. Having a female breadwinner doesn't work for every family, but it makes sense for many. Define your partnership any way you choose, any way that works for you. Take pride in your choices. Defend your right to do things a different way. Your willingness to buck tradition and brave social censure holds potential benefits not only for your children and your marriage but also for society as a whole. It won't always be easy, but remember this: There is strength in numbers, and your ranks are swelling by the day. As more and more women achieve positions of economic power, they will commit to making a political difference not only for their own sake but for the sake of their children. When men and women can accept that they are more similar than different and that their goals—a healthy, happy family life—are the same, they'll be more likely to make progress toward solving their work and family conflicts, from who does the housework to how they can encourage their workplaces to institute more family-friendly policies. And when many voices are raised in unison, change happens.

As the children of today's breadwinners grow to adulthood, raised with the knowledge that men can be nurturing and women can be providers, the world may begin to look different than it does today. Imagine a society where "Daddy and Me" classes are as readily available as the current version, where women who stay home and those who work are equally respected for their individual contributions to society, where an image of an aproned person pushing a vacuum has no gender connotations whatsoever. Hold that thought. Nurture it in your own life and in your children's. The subtle (and not so subtle) stirrings of cultural change are already evident, in everything from changing tables in men's bathrooms to day-care facilities in the workplace. Someday soon the unmarked path you're clearing will be a well-traveled road—something everyone (save, perhaps, a stodgy few) accepts as simply another version of normal.

Acknowledgments

I want to express my gratitude to Dr. Wolfgang Pappenheim, my husband of many years, for his deep understanding of the inner lives of people, and the subtleties and complexities of human relations. His knowledge and wisdom have been an important influence in all of my work. I am also grateful for his support and encouragement throughout this project as I am for the support of our daughter, Meghan, who was kind enough to offer her comments and encouragement after her reading of chapter 7, Fast Forward: The Next Generation. My thanks to Ginny Graves, my collaborator and coauthor, who did all the research for this book and went to great pains to protect the privacy and confidentiality of those couples who generously shared their experiences with us. And my thanks to Julie Merberg, our editor at Roundtable Press, who had so graciously invited me to join her in this project and was of enormous help and support and able, amazingly, to turn my writing into something that was satisfying, even to myself. And my thanks also to Jennifer Brehl, our editor at William Morrow for her patience, fortitude, and belief in the book.

I owe much to the writings of my colleagues and cannot even begin to list them all. Nevertheless, I want to mention Dr. Frank Pittman, whose books *Grow Up!: How Taking Responsibility Can Make You a Happy Adult* and *Man Enough* were replete with the author's characteristic good sense and wisdom. I also want to mention *Same Difference* by Rosalind Barnett and Caryl Rivers; *Necessary Losses* by Judith Viorst; *Therapies with Women in Transition,* edited by Jean Sanville and Ellen Bassin Ruderman; *Necessary Dreams* by Anna Fels; and *Can Love Last?* by the late Stephen A. Mitchell.

And special gratitude goes to all of my patients, who taught me so much and who never fail to impress me with their strength and courage and will to make better lives for themselves.

Harriet Pappenheim, L.C.S.W.
December 2004